Benson & Hedges proudly salutes…

the pleasure of American cooking
through this collection of

Recipes from Great American Inns

Logan Inn, New Hope, Pennsylvania

Editorial Consulting by Evan Jones
Photography by William K. Sladcik
Food Styling by Fran Paulson
Produced by William A. Robinson, Inc.

Cover Recipe: Roast Duckling au Poivre Vert from The Inn at Sawmill Farm, West Dover, Vermont.

The food photography in this book is designed to provide ideas for serving the recipes in your home and does not necessarily represent the way the dishes are served in the various inns. In some instances, recipes have been modified slightly for ease of preparation at home.

Published by
Philip Morris Incorporated
for Benson & Hedges
100 Park Avenue
New York, New York 10017

Printed in the United States of America.

i

FOREWORD

For many Americans, some of our most memorable dining pleasures are linked to country inns. The great inns have essential things in common, the peaceful beauty of a rural scene and the sense of well-being that comes from sitting down to unhurried meals that have been specially prepared. The 54 inns selected for *Benson & Hedges presents Recipes from Great American Inns* all reflect these qualities.

They are representative of the growing number of hostelries that are serving wonderful food. Their recipes offer the best of local fare and dishes from other cuisines that have been adapted to regional preferences.

Each selection featured in our book is a celebration of the fare offered by American inns. You will discover New England Clam Chowder with real down-east taste; savor the unusual combination of ingredients in Sour Cream Chicken Enchiladas that harken back to the Southwest's Spanish settlers; awaken your appetite with Roasted Red Snapper prepared California-style with zestful fresh herbs; find Country Ham with Red-Eye Gravy a Deep South classic worthy of your best brunch.

In the bringing together of these and dozens more American inns specialties, our newest Benson & Hedges book is unique. Each of these very special recipes, we are sure, can bring you dining pleasure for years to come.

Bon Appetit!

CONTENTS

The Lyme Inn, Lyme, New Hampshire

Jared Coffin House

Scallops Sautéed
with Herbs and Vegetables

Jared Coffin House

Nantucket Island, Massachusetts

The Yankee architecture of this island inn takes Nantucket visitors back to the days of sail, as does the hospitality of innkeepers Peggy and Phil Read. Opened as a hotel almost a century ago, Jared Coffin House reflects the grace and charm of those days, with tables set with Wedgwood china and pistol-handled silverware. This tradition is carried further with succulent New England meals accented by recipes brought from the four corners of the world.

On a menu that begins with Quahog Chowder, there may also appear braised veal with eggplant, fried trout in a Scandinavian cream sauce, or duck steak grandmother style.

The inn's Scallops Sautéed with Herbs and Vegetables is outstanding. This saltwater favorite, abounding with tiny bay scallops, is subtly flavored with a colorful assortment of herbs and finely cut vegetables. The result is a delicious Nantucket specialty that satisfies hearty appetites just as it pleases those who choose to eat lightly.

SCALLOPS SAUTÉED WITH HERBS AND VEGETABLES

¼ cup each julienne strips of leeks, carrots, celery, and fennel, if available
2 tablespoons butter
½ cup dry white wine
2 pounds bay scallops or sea scallops cut in thirds (4 cups)
¼ cup butter
1 teaspoon finely chopped sorrel or spinach
1 teaspoon finely chopped parsley
1 teaspoon each finely chopped fresh or ½ teaspoon each dried tarragon or basil leaves
1 large clove garlic, crushed
¼ teaspoon salt
⅛ teaspoon pepper
1 teaspoon all-purpose flour
1 tablespoon soft butter
6 puff pastry shells

Stir-fry the julienne vegetables in a frypan in 2 tablespoons butter for 1 minute; add wine and simmer for 3 minutes. Keep warm. Pat scallops dry. Melt ¼ cup butter in a frypan over medium heat; add scallops. Cook and stir until scallops are almost done, about 3 minutes; add herbs, seasonings and vegetables. Blend flour and soft butter. Push scallops and vegetables to the side of pan; whisk in butter and flour. Cook and stir until slightly thickened. Spoon into puff pastry shells and sprinkle with parsley. Makes 6 servings.

Publick House

Sturbridge, Massachusetts

A blueberry patch and a thriving garden of vegetables help one to envision the Publick House as it must have been in 1771. Inn-keeper Buddy Adler is proud that his hostelry is on the National Register of Historic Places, and he further emphasizes Yankee tradition with such tempting heritage dishes as red flannel hash and deep-dish apple pie. His New England Clam Chowder, exhilarating as a sea breeze, is served with warm, crisp corn sticks, and invites requests for seconds.

NEW ENGLAND CLAM CHOWDER

¼ pound diced salt pork
1 cup diced onion
5 6½-ounce cans minced clams or 2-3 dozen clams
3 medium potatoes, pared and cubed
3 cups light cream
¼ cup butter
½ teaspoon salt
⅛ teaspoon pepper

In a 3- or 4-quart saucepan, cook salt pork over medium heat to render fat; remove crack-lings and reserve. Pour off all but 2 tablespoons fat; add onion and cook until golden. Drain canned clams; reserve. Add clam juice to onions with potatoes. If using fresh clams, wash thor-oughly. Put in a large pot or steamer. Add water to a depth of 1 or 2 inches. Cover and steam until top clams are barely open. Take off heat. Remove clams from shells and chop. Strain liquid and proceed as directed, using 2 to 2½ cups clam broth. Bring onion-and-potato mixture to a boil; cook until potatoes are tender, about 10 minutes. Add chopped clams, cream, butter, reserved cracklings and seasonings. Heat but do not boil. Serve with corn sticks. Makes 8 servings.

Griswold Inn

Veal Birds Griswold and Cheddar Cheese Grits Soufflés

Griswold Inn

Essex, Connecticut

The village of Essex is a port of call for those who love the sea, and "the Gris," as friends affectionately refer to this Early American inn, is the goal of many in search of the tastes of New England. It lured a New York banker named William Winterer back to buy the Griswold and become its history-minded innkeeper.

The tap room has a superlative collection of marine art, and in the library, dining tables are arranged near an antique mural depicting Essex's seafront past. The Steamboat Room duplicates the dining salon of a nineteenth-century side-wheeler.

Featured on Winterer's menus are such delights as fried clams with a unique tartar sauce, "a nest of Canadian quail with bulgur wheat," and smoked pork.

An American colonial favorite offered at the inn is Veal Birds Griswold, wonderfully enhanced by the chef with a succulent stuffing accented by ham, shallots, garlic and rosemary. Serve this colonial dish with individual Cheddar Cheese Grits Soufflés for a meal made elegant by candlelight and the warm company of close friends.

VEAL BIRDS GRISWOLD

2 pounds veal round, cut ¼ inch thick
4 ounces ham, finely chopped (1 cup)
2 tablespoons finely chopped shallots
1 clove garlic, minced
½ teaspoon dried rosemary, crushed
2 tablespoons clarified butter
1 cup white wine
2 cups chicken broth
1 tablespoon cornstarch
2 tablespoons cold water
  Minced parsley

Cut veal into 16 even-sized pieces. Pound each piece to ⅛-inch thickness. Sprinkle with salt and pepper. Combine ham, shallots, garlic and rosemary; top each veal slice with about 1 tablespoon of the mixture. Roll veal around filling and fasten with toothpicks. Melt butter in a large frypan over medium heat; add veal rolls and brown quickly. Add the wine and simmer a few minutes. Add chicken broth; cover and simmer 20 minutes. Remove veal birds to a warm platter. Rapidly boil broth to reduce to about 1½ cups. Combine cornstarch and cold water; stir into hot broth. Cook and stir until slightly thickened. Spoon sauce over veal birds; sprinkle with minced parsley. Makes 8 servings.

Cheddar Cheese Grits Soufflés: Cook 1 cup grits as directed on package. Remove from heat and beat in 2 eggs, one at a time. Stir in 2 cups (8 ounces) shredded sharp Cheddar cheese. Season with a few drops of Tabasco. Turn into eight ⅔-cup or ten ½-cup buttered individual soufflé cups or a buttered 1½-quart casserole or an 8x2-inch round soufflé baking dish. Bake in a 350° oven 30 minutes for cups and 1 hour for large casserole or baking dish. Makes 8-10 servings.

Three Village Inn

Stony Brook, Long Island, New York

Nelson and Monda Roberts' inn is a 24-bedroom colonial house that appeals to various moods with its four dining rooms. Menus emphasize fresh seafood brought in by local fishing boats — bluefish, soft-shell crabs, swordfish and trout. An outstanding light accompaniment to any of these seafoods is Cold Cauliflower Nivernais. As an appetizer or as a salad, these crisp-cooked cauliflowerets, accented with Dijon mustard and garnished with pimiento and parsley, can add sophistication to your next festive dinner.

COLD CAULIFLOWER NIVERNAIS

4 cups cauliflowerets (1 medium)
²/₃ cup mayonnaise
3 tablespoons sour cream
2 tablespoons Dijon mustard
1 tablespoon cream
1 teaspoon lemon juice
  Salt
  Lettuce cups
  Pimiento or red pepper strips
  Chopped parsley

Cook cauliflower in boiling salted water for 5 to 6 minutes. Drain and cool slightly. Combine mayonnaise, sour cream, mustard, cream, lemon juice and salt to taste. Toss with cauliflower and chill. To serve, spoon into lettuce cups and garnish with pimiento and parsley. May be served as an appetizer or salad. Makes 6-8 servings.

Groff's Farm Restaurant
Mt. Joy, Pennsylvania

The unique heritage of Pennsylvania Dutch cooking is always apparent in the abundant meals served by Betty Groff in her handsome eighteenth-century stone farmhouse. Of her many characteristic entrées, her most famous may be creamy, flavorsome Chicken Stoltzfus, a delicately stylish variation of old-fashioned chicken 'n' dumplings.

CHICKEN STOLTZFUS

1 5-pound roasting chicken
6 cups water
1 tablespoon salt
¼ teaspoon pepper
  Pinch saffron
½ cup butter
½ cup all-purpose flour
1 cup light cream
¼ cup minced parsley
  Pastry Squares (See below)

Put chicken, without giblets, into a large pot; add water to almost cover. Add salt, pepper and saffron to water. Bring to a boil; reduce heat; cover and simmer for 1 hour or until chicken is done. Let stand until cool enough to remove skin and bones. Cut chicken meat into bite-size pieces (about 6 cups); set aside. Strain chicken stock; skim and return to pan; boil rapidly to reduce to 4 cups. Melt butter in a large saucepan; stir in flour. Cook and stir until mixture is golden and bubbly, about 5 minutes. Add reduced chicken stock and cream, stirring constantly. Cook and stir until mixture boils. Simmer until thick and smooth. Add chicken and minced parsley. Serve hot over pastry squares. Makes 9-10 servings. *Pastry Squares:* Roll prepared pastry mix as directed on package. Cut into 1-inch squares. Bake in a 375° oven for 12 minutes or until lightly browned.

13

Boone Tavern Hotel and Dining Room

Berea, Kentucky

Just 40 miles south of Lexington in the southern Appalachians, this 60-room inn is an integral part of Berea College and the picturesque community. Thousands of travelers each year go out of their way to sample such palate-tempting dishes as hot spoon bread, chicken with sweet-pepper relish, and blackberry dumplings with milk dip. One special recipe that deserves your repeating often is the Spiced Cranberry Rolls. These puffy dinner rolls are tangy with the sweet bite of cranberries, cinnamon, nutmeg and ginger.

SPICED CRANBERRY ROLLS

            1 package active dry yeast
       ½ cup warm water (105° to 115°)
       ½ cup milk
       ⅓ cup sugar
       ⅓ cup butter
            1 teaspoon salt
4-4½ cups all-purpose flour
            1 teaspoon cinnamon
       ½ teaspoon each ginger and nutmeg
            1 egg
            1 cup chopped cranberries
            2 tablespoons sugar

Soften yeast in warm water. Scald milk. Add ⅓ cup sugar, butter and salt; cool to luke-warm. Put mixture in large bowl. Add 2 cups flour, spices, egg and yeast; beat until smooth. Mix cranberries and 2 tablespoons sugar; add to dough. Stir in flour. Turn out onto a floured surface. Knead until smooth and elastic, add-ing flour as needed. Place in a greased bowl; turn to coat top. Cover and let rise until double. Shape into 48 small balls. Arrange in a greased baking pan. Cover and let rise until doubled. Bake in a 375° oven 20-25 minutes.

The Inn at Sawmill Farm

Roast Duckling au Poivre Vert

The Inn at Sawmill Farm

West Dover, Vermont

In southern Vermont's rustic Mount Snow
Valley The Inn at Sawmill Farm is a nineteenth-
century hill farm imaginatively converted into
a secluded country retreat. Combining the
charm of the past with contemporary lifestyle,
the decor varies from suite to suite, and the
dining rooms have a distinctively Early American feeling of spaciousness and comfort.

Chef Brill Williams, son of innkeepers
Rodney and Ione Williams, offers an eclectic
menu – a farmhouse terrine of meats, an
appetizer combining Vermont cheese and
country ham with asparagus, seasonal
vegetables from nearby gardens and homemade pies of local berries.

The inn's graciously served dinners
underscore the Williams' family talent for
hospitality. Among the noteworthy dishes they
offer is Roast Duckling au Poivre Vert, their
own version of duck enhanced by green
peppercorns. A crisp brown skin contrasts
with the succulently tender meat in this
palate-refreshing main course.

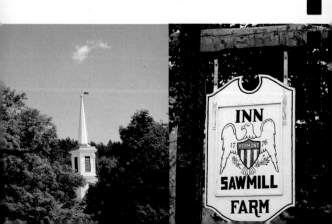

INN

17 VERMONT 76

SAWMILL

FARM

ROAST DUCKLING AU POIVRE VERT

2 5-6-pound roasted ducklings
3 tablespoons chopped shallots
2 tablespoons green peppercorns in vinegar
¼ cup brandy
1 cup white wine
3 tablespoons pan drippings or butter
1½ cups rich veal or beef stock
1 teaspoon salt
2 teaspoons arrowroot or cornstarch
1 tablespoon cold water
1 tablespoon whipping cream

Keep roasted ducklings warm. In a saucepan, combine shallots, 1 tablespoon peppercorns, brandy, wine, pan drippings; bring to a boil; reduce to about ¾ cup. Add veal stock, remaining peppercorns, salt; bring to a boil. Combine arrowroot, cold water; whisk into sauce. Boil to reduce sauce to 1 cup; whisk in cream. Cut duckling in half. Under broiler, crisp skin and heat. Serve with peppercorn sauce, English Dressing. Makes 4 servings.

English Dressing: Melt ½ cup butter in a saucepan, add 3 tablespoons grated onion; simmer 5 minutes. Remove crust from 10 slices of bread and cut into cubes; add to butter and onion, mixing until butter is absorbed. Add ½ cup whipping cream, ½ teaspoon salt and 1 tablespoon parsley; mix thoroughly.

Wayside Inn Since 1797

Middletown, Virginia

Bed-and-board has been a sweet reward extended by this Shenandoah coach stop since George Washington's time. Colonial themes prevail in architecture and decor, and menus feature regional dishes: mountain cured ham, pan-fried chicken and Shenandoah apple pie. Many meals begin with a cup of Wayside Inn Peanut Soup to whet the appetite. This Southern classic takes only minutes to prepare and is very festive topped with chopped peanuts.

WAYSIDE INN PEANUT SOUP

    3 cups chicken broth
    1 cup peanut butter
    ⅛ teaspoon celery salt
    ⅛ teaspoon onion salt
    ⅛ teaspoon sugar
    1⅓ cups cream or 1 13-ounce can evaporated milk
      Chopped peanuts

Heat chicken broth to boiling; add peanut butter, stirring until smooth. Season to taste with celery salt and onion salt. Add sugar. Stir in cream or evaporated milk. Heat; do not boil. Top with chopped peanuts. Makes 6 servings.

Colonial Inn

Hillsborough, North Carolina

Located in the foothills of the Piedmonts between Greensboro and Durham, the Colonial Inn offers North Carolina cooking at its best. Visitors to this stately inn will find a bill of fare which includes Brunswick stew, chicken and dumplings, fried okra and tangy green tomato pie. The inn also proudly serves Country Ham with Red-Eye Gravy, an American classic with Deep South appeal that can add pungent enhancement when you offer it at home, especially when accompanied with Hush Puppies.

COUNTRY HAM WITH RED-EYE GRAVY

6 ¼-inch slices country ham or other well-smoked ham
¼ cup margarine
¼ cup packed brown sugar
½ cup strong black coffee

In a heavy frypan, sauté ham in margarine until light brown, turning several times. Remove ham from pan and keep warm. Stir brown sugar into pan drippings; cook over low heat, stirring constantly, until sugar melts. Add coffee; simmer and stir 5 minutes until mixture is a rich red-brown color. Serve ham slices with gravy and Hush Puppies. Makes 6 servings.

Hush Puppies: Combine 1 cup yellow cornmeal, 1 cup biscuit mix or self-rising flour, 1 tablespoon sugar and ¼ teaspoon baking powder in a mixing bowl. Add ½ cup water, ¼ cup evaporated milk or cream, 1 beaten egg and 1 tablespoon cooking oil (add 2 tablespoons cooking oil, if using self-rising flour) to cornmeal mixture and mix well. Let stand 10 minutes. Drop by tablespoons into deep hot fat (360°) and fry until golden brown. Makes 12 large or 18 medium puppies.

Pine Crest Inn

Tryon, North Carolina

On a pine ridge in fox hunting country, the Pine Crest Inn offers relaxation and good Southern food typical of a Blue Ridge country estate. Guests may be served by candlelight with entrées such as crisp roast duck with the inn's cranberry-orange relish. Or, they may help themselves from the many appealing buffet selections, which often include an outstanding Chicken and Rice Ring with Mushroom Sauce. This recipe, in which simplicity and a winning balance of flavors are present, is equally at home as dinner fare.

CHICKEN AND RICE RING WITH MUSHROOM SAUCE

    8 cups diced cooked chicken (about 2½ pounds)
    2 cups cooked rice (follow package directions)
    4 cups soft bread crumbs
       4-ounce jar pimientos, chopped (½ cup)
    8 eggs, well beaten
 1½ cups chicken broth
 1½ teaspoons salt
    1 teaspoon paprika
    ⅛ teaspoon each dried rosemary and marjoram
    ½ cup melted butter or chicken fat
    6 cups canned mushroom sauce

Combine chicken, cooked rice, bread crumbs and pimientos in a large mixing bowl. Beat together eggs, chicken broth and seasonings; pour over chicken mixture with melted butter. Toss to mix thoroughly. Grease a 12-cup or two 6-cup ring molds. Cut foil strips and line mold for easier unmolding. Grease foil. Turn chicken mixture into mold. Place in a pan of hot water. Bake in a 325° oven for 45-60 minutes. Let stand 10 minutes; unmold on a large platter; remove foil. Serve with mushroom sauce. Makes 12 servings.

L'Hostellerie Bressane

Glacé Red Raspberry Soufflé

L'Hostellerie Bressane

Hillsdale, New York

Once a coach stop west of the Berkshires, this red brick house was transformed when Jean and Madeleine Morel moved from Manhattan to establish a rural restaurant on a par with the best in the U.S. The five rooms upstairs are frequently reserved for "overnighting" by guests who know the exceptional pleasure of eating downstairs in one of the small, stylish dining rooms.

Chef Morel named his inn for the French region of Bresse, which is famous for cornfed chickens. In addition to poultry dishes, he has become famous for Hudson River shad with sorrel sauce, broiled lobster in garlic butter and sweetbreads in port wine with chestnuts.

A perfect ending for a meal prepared by Chef Morel, or for dinner at home, is this Glacé Red Raspberry Soufflé. It is a simply turned-out dessert made almost regal by the color and flavor of ripe, red berries. This is a dish you can prepare in advance of your dinner party because it keeps perfectly for several days in the freezer.

GLACÉ RED RASPBERRY SOUFFLÉ

2 10-ounce packages frozen raspberries or 1 pint
   fresh raspberries plus 2 tablespoons sugar
¾ cup sugar
⅓ cup water
6 eggs, separated
2 cups whipping cream, whipped

Over low heat, cook raspberries until liquid is
almost gone (about 15 minutes). Set aside to
cool. Combine sugar and water in a medium
saucepan; bring to a boil and boil rapidly for 3
minutes to soft ball stage (240°). In a small
mixer bowl, beat egg yolks until thick and
lemon colored. With mixer on medium speed,
slowly pour hot syrup over egg yolks; beat
until thick and light. Fold in raspberries. Beat
egg whites until stiff peaks form. Fold into
raspberry mixture. Fold in whipped cream.
Tape 2-inch standing collars of aluminum foil
around 8 individual soufflé dishes or cups.
Spoon raspberry mixture in, filling to top of
collar. Freeze. Remove collar to serve. Garnish
with whipped cream and a fresh raspberry.
Makes 8 servings.

New Jefferson Inn

Jefferson, Texas

The New Jefferson Inn, with its Victorian decor, is a high point for visitors to the restored town of Jefferson. Innkeeper "Red" Fisher's weekend dinners are as memorable as the Alamo. A Texas favorite is the peppery Shrimp Gumbo made succulent with tomatoes, garlic, okra, and Southern seasonings. At home, you can make this gumbo with okra alone, or with filé powder, the sassafras compound first used by Louisiana Indians in native stews.

SHRIMP GUMBO

    4 quarts water
    2 ounces shrimp-crab boil (¼ cup)
2½ pounds peeled and deveined shrimp
    3 tablespoons each butter and bacon fat
    1 cup each diced celery, onion and green pepper
    1 28-ounce can tomatoes
    1 teaspoon dried thyme
    1 clove garlic, minced
    1 bay leaf
    1 teaspoon Worcestershire sauce
    1 tablespoon gumbo filé powder
    1 teaspoon salt
    ½ teaspoon pepper
    1 10-ounce package frozen cut okra, defrosted
    ¼ cup rice

In a large pot, bring 4 quarts water to a boil. Tie shrimp boil in a cheesecloth bag. Add to the boiling water with the shrimp. Bring to a boil, reduce heat and simmer 10 minutes. Turn off heat and let stand 10 minutes. Drain shrimp, reserving 2 cups stock. Put butter and bacon fat in a Dutch oven; add celery, onion and green pepper. Cook until tender. Add 2 cups shrimp stock, tomatoes, thyme, garlic, bay leaf, Worcestershire sauce, filé powder, salt and pepper; simmer 45 minutes. Add shrimp, okra and rice; simmer 30 minutes or until rice is tender. Makes 6-8 servings.

Squire Tarbox Inn

Wiscasset, Maine

Off the beaten path in a quiet section on the Maine coast, the Tarbox has accommodations of only six rooms, but travelers who cannot stay the night still can partake of the inn's bountiful dinners. The cooking here is distinguished by vegetables freshly picked from the inn gardens to accompany fresh Maine seafood. Dinners end resoundingly with innkeeper Anne McInvale's old-fashioned country desserts served warm from the oven. Among such comforts is this summer-kitchen gingerbread, bursting with blueberries, which doubles as a very special brunch treat.

BLUEBERRY GINGERBREAD

½ cup cooking oil
1 cup sugar
½ teaspoon salt
3 tablespoons molasses
1 egg
2 cups all-purpose flour
½ teaspoon ginger
1 teaspoon cinnamon
½ teaspoon nutmeg
1 teaspoon baking soda
1 cup fresh or frozen blueberries
1 cup buttermilk
2 tablespoons sugar

With electric mixer, beat together oil, 1 cup sugar, salt and molasses; beat in egg. Combine flour, spices and baking soda; dredge blueberries with 2 tablespoons of flour mixture. Add remaining flour mixture to first mixture alternately with buttermilk, beating after each addition. Stir in blueberries. Pour into a greased and floured 12x7½x2-inch baking dish. Sprinkle top with remaining sugar. Bake in a 350° oven for 35-40 minutes. Cut into squares and serve warm with butter. May be served with whipped cream for dessert. Makes 12 servings.

veal
picatta
wild rice
butternut
squash
green salad
lemon tarts

City Hotel

Columbia, California

Near Yosemite National Park and a cheery morning's drive from San Francisco, the town of Columbia is now under historical restoration. Here, the City Hotel has revived Gold Rush hospitality to provide both lodging and a fine dining room. Chef Barry Marcillac adds his own touch to blue-ribbon veal specialties. His Fettine de Vitello Piccata presents tender veal medallions in a wine sauce, gently spiked with lemon and shallots, and is easy on the calories.

FETTINE DE VITELLO PICCATA

    2 pounds veal tenderloin, cut into 3-ounce pieces
    ⅓ cup all-purpose flour
6-8 tablespoons butter
    ¼ teaspoon salt
    ⅛ teaspoon white pepper
    ¾ cup dry white wine
    2 tablespoons minced shallots
    1 tablespoon lemon juice
    2 teaspoons minced parsley
    ½ cup butter, chilled

Pound veal pieces until very thin. Dip both sides in flour, shaking off excess. Heat 3 tablespoons butter in a frypan over medium heat. Quickly sauté a few pieces at a time, turning to lightly brown both sides; add butter as needed. Remove meat; keep warm on a heated platter. When all veal is cooked, season with salt and pepper. Pour excess butter out of pan; add wine, shallots and lemon juice; reduce to one-third. Take off heat. Add parsley and ½ cup butter, quickly and lightly blending with a small whip to a creamy texture. Pour sauce over veal. Serve immediately. Makes 6-8 servings of 3 pieces each.

Stonehenge

Ridgefield, Connecticut

Reflected in its own trout pond, the country house known as Stonehenge is impressively framed by gardens and a handful of room-service cottages. But guests are even more impressed by its cuisine, which emphasizes classics like roast pheasant with champagne kraut, roast saddle of venison with apples, and lingonberries with chestnuts. A delightful ending to a Stonehenge repast is this scrumptious Chocolate Whiskey Cake, laced with bourbon and so rich with chocolate, raisins, and almonds, it is almost a confection.

STONEHENGE CHOCOLATE WHISKEY CAKE

½ cup seedless raisins
⅔ cup bourbon whiskey
1 cup sugar
¼ cup water
10 1-ounce squares unsweetened chocolate, cut up
¾ cup butter
6 eggs, separated
1 cup ground blanched almonds
½ cup flour

Soak raisins in whiskey. Boil sugar and water together. Add chocolate; remove from heat and stir until chocolate melts; cool. With electric mixer, beat butter until softened. Beat in egg yolks, one at a time. With mixer on low speed, add half the chocolate mixture, then half the ground almonds. Repeat. Add whiskey and raisins; beat in flour. Beat egg whites until stiff. Fold beaten egg whites into batter. Line bottom of a 9-inch tube spring-form pan with wax paper; grease and flour. Bake in a 375° oven for 30 minutes. Frost if desired.

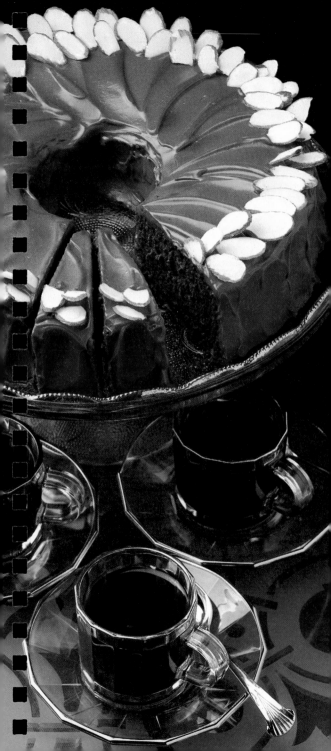

Longfellow House

Pascagoula, Mississippi

On the Gulf of Mexico shore, halfway between Mobile and Gulfport, the majestic antebellum Longfellow House symbolizes Southern hospitality, as do its menus. They are enriched with seafood only minutes old, and desserts, many of which were originated by the chef. Among the dessert specialties is this sinfully tempting Sweet Edna Lou. It is a layered confection composed of filled tarts smothered under whipped cream, chocolate syrup and pecans. You will find it easy to make and impressive to serve.

SWEET EDNA LOU

Prepared pastry for two-crust pie
1 4½-ounce package instant chocolate pudding mix
1 4½-ounce package instant vanilla pudding mix
3 cups cold milk
1 8-ounce package whipped cream cheese, warm
1 cup whipping cream, whipped
2 tablespoons confectioners sugar
½ teaspoon vanilla
Pecan pieces
Chocolate syrup

On a lightly floured surface, roll pastry ⅛ inch thick; cut into 10 5½-inch circles, rerolling scraps as needed. Fit into 10 3½-inch tart pans; crimp edges and prick bottoms with a fork. Bake in a 425° oven for 8-10 minutes or until brown. Cool. Combine the 2 pudding mixes; beat in 3 cups cold milk as directed on the package. When pudding thickens, spoon ⅓ cupful into each tart shell. Chill until firm, 1 to 2 hours. Carefully spread softened whipped cream cheese over pudding. Refrigerate until serving time. Sweeten whipped cream with confectioners sugar and vanilla. Spoon over cream cheese. Sprinkle with pecan pieces and drizzle with chocolate syrup. Makes 8-10 servings.

35

Chadwick's Restaurant South Seas Plantation

Captiva Island, Florida

One of Florida's best restaurants occupies a refurbished key-lime warehouse near Captiva Island's plantation house – a thirty-mile drive from Fort Myers. The deluxe menu features such seafood specialties as Puff 'N' Stuff Balls, an unusual presentation of crabmeat. The delectable balls are dipped in flour-and-beer batter to be deep-fried and served with crab claws and fish fillets for a mouth-watering dinner catch.

PUFF 'N' STUFF BALLS

1 pound cooked crabmeat, finely chopped
¼ cup each minced celery, onion and carrot
½ teaspoon pepper
¼ teaspoon paprika
¾ cup all-purpose flour
½ teaspoon paprika
¼ teaspoon white pepper
1 teaspoon salt
2 eggs, separated
¾ cup beer
2 tablespoons oil
   Fat for deep frying

Combine crab with minced vegetables, ½ teaspoon pepper, ¼ teaspoon paprika. Shape into small balls. Cover and refrigerate. Combine flour, ½ teaspoon paprika, ¼ teaspoon white pepper and 1 teaspoon salt. Add egg yolks, beer and oil; whisk until smooth. Cover bowl and refrigerate 2 hours or overnight. Beat egg whites until stiff peaks form. Stir batter and fold in egg whites. Using 2 forks, carefully roll crab balls in batter. Fry in deep hot fat (350°) until brown, about 2 minutes. Drain on paper towel. Shrimp, crab claws, fish pieces and vegetables may be dipped in batter and fried to serve with crab balls. Makes 2 dozen.

The Lyme Inn

Lyme, New Hampshire

Ten miles up the Connecticut River from
Dartmouth College, Lyme is one of those
pretty colonial New Hampshire villages, and
the inn is characteristic of Yankee taverns
dedicated to food and rest. The kitchen
features excellent seafood, special garden
casseroles, and New England desserts.
A popular specialty is the inn's Hasenpfeffer,
which offers the traveler a truly old-fashioned
rabbit stew with subtle spicy flavors brought
to a peak through two days of marinating.

HASENPFEFFER

2 rabbits, cut up (about 5-6 pounds) or chicken
1 recipe wine marinade (See below)
1½ cups diced onion
1 cup small or quartered mushrooms
4 slices bacon, cut up
3-4 tablespoons butter
2 teaspoons salt
½ cup all-purpose flour
½ cup sour cream

Marinate rabbit for 2 days in wine marinade
made from 2 cups wine, 1 cup water, ½ cup
vinegar, 1 tablespoon lemon juice, 12 peppercorns, 4 cloves garlic, ½ teaspoon each thyme,
rosemary, marjoram leaves and 1 cup celery
leaves. Keep refrigerated.

In a large Dutch oven, cook onions, mushrooms and bacon until onions are soft. Lift out
vegetables and bacon. Add 3 or 4 tablespoons
butter to pan. Lift rabbit out of marinade; pat
dry. Strain marinade. Sprinkle salt over rabbit;
dip in flour; brown in butter. When all rabbit is
brown, return with onion mixture to pan; pour
strained marinade over rabbit and vegetables.
Cover and simmer until tender, about 1 hour.
Lift rabbit onto a heated platter. Stir salt and
flour into sour cream; add to sauce in pan;
spoon over rabbit. Makes 8 servings.

Sherman House

Batesville, Indiana

On the far eastern border of Indiana, the Sherman House abuts Ohio and Kentucky and attracts diners from these states with its varied fare. It's not often one finds an establishment equally renowned for country food such as crunchy fried chicken, and for continental cuisine such as Beef Wellington. Next time you give an elegant dinner, prepare the Sherman House's Wellington recipe for individual beef tenderloins. They are topped with liver pâté and a mushroom-shallot mixture, and served in their own golden-baked puff pastry "envelopes." Or for a buffet party, offer a whole tenderloin presented in this extraordinary manner.

BEEF WELLINGTON

4 6-ounce portions trimmed beef tenderloin
2 tablespoons butter
4 teaspoons finely chopped shallots
½ pound mushrooms, finely chopped (2 cups)
1 tablespoon Burgundy wine
   2½-ounce can chicken or goose liver pâté
   17¼-ounce package frozen puff pastry dough
   (2 9x10-inch sheets), defrosted
1 egg yolk beaten with 1 teaspoon water

Season meat with salt and pepper. In a heavy frypan quickly sear fillets on both sides. Remove from pan and set aside. Turn heat to low; add butter, shallots, mushrooms and wine to pan. Cook and stir until all liquid is gone and mixture is very soft. Spread 1 tablespoon pâté over the top of each fillet; then spread and pat ¼ cup of mushroom mixture over pâté. Carefully wrap each mushroom-topped fillet in pastry rolling pastry to stretch as needed. Pinch edges to seal. Brush with beaten egg yolk. Bake in a 450° oven for 15 minutes. Makes 4 servings.

El Tovar Lodge

Grand Canyon, Arizona

Deep in Grand Canyon country, El Tovar is one of the most acclaimed national park hostelries. Characteristically, its featured entrées include Rocky Mountain trout and game birds prepared in various ways. As a fitting first course, you may order an exquisite light Cantaloupe Mousse peaked with whipped cream. Treating your guests at home to this appetizing confection can be just as rewarding, especially when it is prepared in a pretty fruit mold shape.

CANTALOUPE MOUSSE

½ medium ripe cantaloupe, seeded, pared and
   cut into small pieces
2 envelopes unflavored gelatin (2 tablespoons)
¼ cup cold water
2 cups heavy cream
4 egg whites
2 cups sugar

Purée melon in a blender or food processor. Sprinkle gelatin over cold water to soften; stir over hot water to dissolve. Cool and add to melon. Whip cream until soft peaks form, gradually adding 1 cup sugar. Whip egg whites until fluffy; gradually add remaining sugar and whip until stiff peaks form. Fold cream into egg whites. Add blended cantaloupe and gelatin. Chill 1 hour. Makes 8 servings.

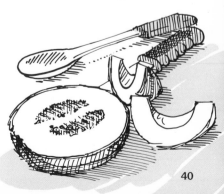

Robert Morris Inn

Oysters à la Gino

Robert Morris Inn

Oxford, Maryland

The original Robert Morris was a Maryland tobacco exporter, and his namesake son was a signer of the Declaration of Independence. The handsome, many-gabled house in which both lived was reputedly built by ships' carpenters so well it still serves to welcome sailors who drop anchor out front in the Tred Avon River. In season the river is a haven for hunters of waterbirds and for fishermen.

This inn, with its historic traditions, is equally well known for its fresh Chesapeake Bay seafood, including lump crabmeat, deep-fried crab cakes, rockfish fillets and famous oyster dishes.

One of the inn's specialties is Oysters à la Gino. An Eastern Shore favorite, this succulent appetizer can bring uncommon style to hearty American fare, or you can make it the featured dish for a special occasion.

OYSTERS À LA GINO

2 tablespoons butter
⅓ cup all-purpose flour
1 tablespoon paprika
½ teaspoon monosodium glutamate
½ teaspoon garlic powder
½ teaspoon Chesapeake Bay-style seafood seasoning
  (if not available, add cayenne to other seafood
  seasoning)
½ teaspoon white pepper
1 cup milk
2 tablespoons Worcestershire sauce
2 tablespoons dry sherry
6 -8 ounces cooked lump crabmeat (about 1 cup)
24 oysters on the half shell
6 slices bacon, cut into 4 pieces

Melt butter in a heavy pan over low heat; mix in flour and dry seasonings. Stir in the milk and Worcestershire sauce; whisk until smooth. Cook until thickened, about 5 minutes, stirring constantly. Remove from heat and add sherry. Cool mixture for 20 minutes. Gently mix in crabmeat. Arrange oysters on a shallow baking pan; top each with a tablespoon of crab mixture. Place a piece of bacon atop each. Bake in a 375° oven for 10 to 12 minutes or until bacon is crisp. Makes 6-8 appetizer servings.

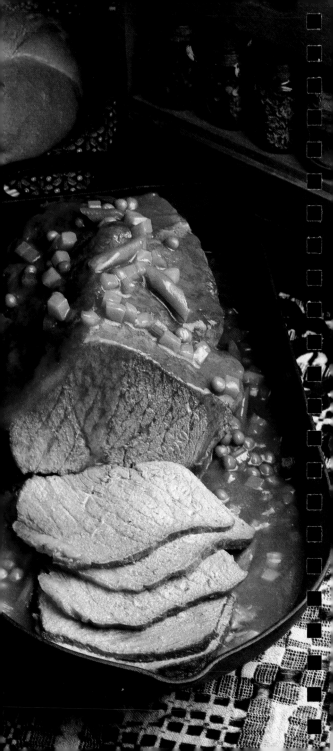

Longfellow's Wayside Inn

Sudbury, Massachusetts

Authentically restored lodgings complement the Colonial Dining Room, in which the menu offers a variety of wholesome Yankee fare. Homemade bread from flour ground in its own gristmill is served with the early New England style meals at this Wayside Inn. A favorite, among dishes such as fresh scrod, beef broth with barley and apple-stuffed roast goose, is a thoroughbred Yankee Pot Roast immersed in a gleaming brown sauce and rich with the earthy flavors of garden vegetables.

YANKEE POT ROAST

¼ pound salt pork or bacon fat
1 4 - 6 pound bottom round roast
2 each medium celery stalks and carrots
1 small onion, sliced
1 1-pound can tomatoes
2 teaspoons salt
6 peppercorns
1 bay leaf
3 cups water
¼ cup flour
⅓ cup each cooked peas, cubed carrots,
    cut string beans
½ cup cooked, chopped celery

In a Dutch oven, brown roast in salt pork or bacon fat. Put celery, carrots, onion and tomatoes around meat. Sprinkle salt, peppercorns and bay leaf over roast; add water. Bring to a boil. Cover and simmer over low heat or in a 350° oven 2½ hours. Lift out roast; keep warm. Strain stock, discarding vegetables. Skim fat off stock, returning ¼ cup fat to Dutch oven; stir flour into fat; add 4 cups stock; cook and stir until thickened. Check seasonings. Add vegetables and heat. Serve gravy with sliced beef. Makes 12-15 servings.

Logan Inn

New Hope, Pennsylvania

For 250 years, wayfarers have paused in New Hope, perhaps the most charming town in Bucks County, and hundreds have felt themselves lucky to put up at the Logan Inn. The inn's recipes are from many ethnic traditions and include cassoulet, chicken Kiev and Bavarian sauerbraten. An out-of-the-ordinary main dish is the Logan version of Chicken Livers Romanoff, which is easily duplicated at home and is especially dramatic when layered into a clear casserole.

CHICKEN LIVERS ROMANOFF

　　1 pound chicken livers
　　¼ cup butter
　　1 tablespoon brandy
　　1 tablespoon minced shallots
　　½ pound mushrooms, sliced (about 3 cups)
　　1 tablespoon all-purpose flour
1 ½ cups sour cream
　　1 recipe each Rice and Spinach Layers (See below)

If chicken livers are large, cut in half; sprinkle with salt and pepper. Sauté in ¼ cup butter until pink; add brandy. Remove from pan; keep warm. Add shallots to butter in pan; cook until tender. Add mushrooms; cook 1 minute. Stir flour into sour cream; quickly mix with mushrooms in pan. Return livers to sauce and heat. *Rice Layer:* Sauté ½ cup onion in ¼ cup butter until soft; add 1 cup long grain rice and cook and stir 2 to 3 minutes or until rice begins to brown. Add 2 cups hot chicken broth; stir. Cover tightly and simmer 15-20 minutes or until broth is absorbed. Keep warm.

Spinach Layer: Prepare two packages frozen creamed spinach. Season with nutmeg. Keep warm. Layer into 3-quart casserole as follows: spinach, rice and liver mixture. Heat, uncovered, in a 350° oven 15 minutes. Serves 6.

The Bird & Bottle Inn

Black Bean Soup

The Bird & Bottle Inn

Garrison, New York

The huge fireplace and the wide pine floor-
boards in the dining room identify The Bird
& Bottle as a colonial mansion exceptionally
well restored. Upstairs are two double rooms
and two suites, but it is in the dining room,
shining with silver, crystal, china and white
linen, that Bird & Bottle standards are most
apparent. The house was built in 1761 and
became an inn in 1940, earning its reputation
among gourmets when innkeeper Tom
Noonan took command.

In the kitchen, troutlets are prepared as
appetizers, rack of lamb is surrounded by
broiled tomatoes, and desserts range from
Jamaica rum mousse to apple almond tarts.

A great way to start a meal at The Bird
& Bottle is with Tom Noonan's Black Bean
Soup. This exotic yet fortifying dish has been
favored by Americans since clipper-ship days.
It is so nourishing that it makes a wonderful
meal in itself, especially when accompanied
by a green salad and a light dessert.

BLACK BEAN SOUP

12-ounce package black turtle beans
2½ quarts cold water (10 cups)
1 cup chopped celery
2 cups chopped onion
¼ cup butter
4 teaspoons all-purpose flour
¼ cup chopped parsley
Rind and bone from smoked ham
2 medium leeks, thinly sliced (about ¾ cup)
2 bay leaves
1½ teaspoons salt
¼ teaspoon pepper
½ cup dry Madeira or sherry

Wash and pick through beans. Cover with boiling water and soak overnight. Drain and put in a large soup pot; add cold water. Cover, bring to a boil and cook over low heat for 1½ hours. In a frypan, slowly cook celery and onion in butter. Blend in flour and parsley; stir in 2 cups beans and liquid. Add to remaining bean mixture. Stir to mix. Add rind and bone, leeks, bay leaves, salt and pepper. Cover and simmer 2½ hours or until beans are cooked. Discard rind, bone and bay leaves. Drain beans, reserving broth, and put through a sieve or food mill. Return to broth; stir in Madeira and heat. Float a lemon slice and sprinkle chopped hard cooked egg on each serving. Makes 8-10 servings.

Chalet Suzanne Restaurant & Inn

Lake Wales, Florida

The Chalet Suzanne's striking interiors and excellent cuisine make it one of the finest places in Florida to stop for food and lodging. Menu choices range from their famous broiled grapefruit topped by sautéed chicken livers to crêpes Suzanne accented by the Chalet's unique sauce. A special appetizer often used for hors d'oeuvres at private parties is this Roquefort Mousse Dean. Simple to make, it can add glamour to any occasion and is delightful served with bite-size, low-calorie raw vegetables.

ROQUEFORT MOUSSE DEAN

1½ envelopes unflavored gelatin (1½ tablespoons)
¼ cup cold water
6 egg yolks
2 cups whipping cream
¾ pound Roquefort or blue cheese
3 egg whites, stiffly beaten
2 tablespoons poppy seeds

Sprinkle gelatin over cold water to soften. Combine egg yolks and ½ cup of cream in a small heavy saucepan. Over low heat, cook and beat with a whisk until mixture is creamy and slightly thickened. Add gelatin and beat until dissolved. Pour into a large mixing bowl and set aside. Press cheese through a sieve or process in a blender or food processor until smooth; add to gelatin mixture. Cool until mixture is partially set. Whip remaining cream and fold into cheese mixture; then fold in egg whites and poppy seeds. Turn mixture into an oiled 2-quart mold. Chill. To serve, unmold on serving plate. Garnish with endive and serve with raw vegetable crudités, toast rounds and crackers. Makes about 35 appetizer servings.

Old Drovers Inn

Dover Plains, New York

For those who turn off N.Y. Route 22 for lunch
or dinner, the Old Drovers offers American
fare that transcends time. On the blackboard
menu are Cheddar soup, game bird pâté,
a colonial lamb curry and raspberry sherbet.
But nothing may be more typically American
than the inn's Browned Turkey Hash. It is a
hearty, economical dish to prepare with
ease in your own kitchen, and becomes
especially memorable when served with a
zesty Mustard Sauce.

BROWNED TURKEY HASH

1½ cups medium diced cooked turkey white meat
2½ cups medium diced cooked turkey dark meat
 1 cup finely diced boiled potatoes
 4 tablespoons finely chopped onion, optional
 ¼ to ½ cup clarified butter
 ¼ teaspoon paprika
   Chopped parsley

Mix ingredients in bowl; salt and pepper to
taste. Heat ¼ cup butter in a well-seasoned
or release-coated 7-inch frypan until it begins
to brown; stir in paprika. Quickly add turkey
mixture and pack it firmly on bottom and sides
of pan. Cover and reduce heat to medium.
Cook 5-7 minutes or until edges brown, adding more butter if necessary. Turn out onto
a heated plate. Sprinkle a few crystals of
monosodium glutamate over top, if desired.
Garnish with chopped parsley.

Mustard Sauce: Combine 3 cups chicken
stock, ½ cup beef consommé, 2 tablespoons
Coleman's dry yellow mustard and ½ cup
prepared Dijon mustard. Beat with a whisk to
blend. Thicken with equal parts butter and
flour; cooking and stirring until consistency
of heavy cream. Serve very hot on top or on
side of hash. Makes 1 quart.

Erich's

Austin, Texas

It is the Viennese cuisine that draws Austinites to this intimate country cottage restaurant west of the city. Although pastries may be Erich's forte, entrées, such as his delectable Wiener-Kalbs Goulash are not to be over-looked. This Austrian veal stew is a taste triumph which you can recreate at home for your best friends, then serve with a side dish of spaetzle or other favorite pasta.

WIENER-KALBS GOULASH

1 cup butter
4 cups chopped onions
⅓ cup Hungarian paprika
2 tablespoons tomato paste
1 teaspoon salt
4 cups veal or chicken stock
3 cloves garlic, mashed
3 bay leaves
½ lemon with peel
5 pounds veal shanks
3 tablespoons all-purpose flour
1 cup whipping cream

Melt butter in a Dutch oven; add onion and cook until golden brown. Remove from heat and stir in paprika, tomato paste and salt; mix well. Add veal stock, garlic, bay leaves and lemon. Remove meat from bones and cut into 1½-inch chunks. (You should have about 3 pounds.) Add meat to mixture. Bring to a boil, reduce heat, cover and simmer 1 hour, until tender. Using a slotted spoon, lift meat and seasonings from sauce; discard lemon and bay leaves. Process sauce in a blender or food processor until smooth; return to Dutch oven and heat to boiling. Mix flour and 3 table-spoons cream until smooth; stir into hot sauce with remaining cream. Cook and stir until thickened. Add meat and heat. Serve with noodles or spaetzle. Makes 8-10 servings.

The Carriage House

Fort Worth, Texas

Those who know there is more to the Lone Star State's culinary range than prime steaks, chili, and barbecue habitually drive out Camp Bowie Boulevard for The Carriage House's continental dining. A house favorite is their salads served with Mr. Mac's Salad Dressing, the innkeeper's own special recipe. Its unusual zest comes from half a dozen spicy ingredients blended with safflower oil and lemon juice, which elegantly dresses crisp mixed greens or a salad of spinach and mushrooms.

MR. MAC'S SALAD DRESSING

2 cups safflower oil
1 cup fresh lemon juice
1 teaspoon packaged seasoned pepper
½ teaspoon salt
½ teaspoon dry mustard
1 teaspoon pepper, fresh ground
⅛ teaspoon monosodium glutamate
1 tablespoon Worcestershire sauce
   Dash Tabasco
¼ cup minced onion
1 hard-cooked egg, minced

Put all ingredients in a blender or food processor. Process to blend. Refrigerate over-night to blend flavors. Serve over mixed salad greens or spinach and mushroom salad. Makes 3½ cups.

Schumacher's New Prague Hotel

New Prague, Minnesota

Twelve festively decorated lodging rooms named after the months of the year establish the European mood created by John and Nancy Schumacher. Some fifty-five main dishes created by Chef John enhance that mood. Cooked to order, and prepared with Czech flair, they include walleye pike garnished with caraway and a delicious appetizer called Escargots à la Nancy. These mushroom caps stuffed with snails and, surprisingly, tiny bay scallops take only minutes to prepare and set the stage for a gala meal.

ESCARGOTS À LA NANCY

16 large mushrooms
½ cup butter (¼ pound)
 1 tablespoon crumbled cooked bacon (3 slices)
½ teaspoon minced shallots
½ teaspoon chopped parsley
½ teaspoon garlic powder or 1 clove garlic, minced
16 bay scallops (4 ounces)
16 snails

Wash and dry mushrooms, removing stems. Put mushrooms in a baking dish, hollow side up. Stir butter to soften; stir in bacon, shallots, parsley and garlic. Put one scallop and one snail in each mushroom cap. Cover with butter mixture, using about 1 rounded teaspoon in each. Bake in a 350° oven for 20-25 minutes. Serve with rye toast points. Makes 4 servings.

Beaumont Inn

Cream of Broccoli Soup

Beaumont Inn

Harrodsburg, Kentucky

Four generations of the Dedman family have greeted guests who enter the Beaumont through the stately white Ionic columns lining the portico. In all that time the inn has been a stout champion of Blue Grass open-heartedness and Southern cooking.

The entrance hall salutes the memory of General Robert E. Lee, a special family hero, and the food served in the formal dining rooms is dominated by Confederacy favorites: hot biscuits stuffed with country cured ham, butterscotch pie, and the South's famous Robert E. Lee Cake.

The same Southern heritage is reflected in this special family recipe for Cream of Broccoli Soup. Served as it might have been in Confederacy days, it is a delectable, delicately flavored beginning for any meal, and it will subtly complement your family favorites.

CREAM OF BROCCOLI SOUP

1½ quarts water (6 cups)
   10-ounce package frozen chopped broccoli
¾ cup finely chopped onion
2 teaspoons salt
2 teaspoons monosodium glutamate
2 teaspoons white pepper
1 teaspoon garlic powder
8 ounces American cheese, shredded (2 cups)
1 cup milk
1 cup cream
¼ cup butter
⅓ cup all-purpose flour
½ cup cold water

In a 3-quart saucepan, bring 1½ quarts water to a boil; add broccoli and onion and boil 10 to 12 minutes. Add seasonings and shredded cheese; stir until cheese melts. Add milk, cream and butter; stir and heat to boiling. Slowly add water to flour, stirring constantly until texture is smooth. Slowly add to hot mixture, stirring rapidly. Cook and stir until soup is the consistency of heavy cream. Makes 8-10 servings.

The Country Inn

Berkeley Springs, West Virginia

In the Old Dominion dining room, with its white walls and dark wood paneling, inn-keeper Bill North emphasizes down-home cooking and manor-house service. The menu includes kitchen-brewed soups of fresh stocks and local vegetables, Appalachian hams, and baked-out-back pies and cakes. On a blustery cold day, as a relaxing prelude to a hearty meal, the innkeeper features two pre-Civil War libations: Hot Buttered Rum afloat with butter and a lemon twist, and a froth-collared Country Inn Apple Sour fortified with applejack and wild cherry brandy.

HOT BUTTERED RUM

        6 cups cider
        3 cinnamon sticks
        4 cloves
        1 lemon slice
    12 ounces golden rum
        4 teaspoons butter
        8 lemon twists

Put cider, cinnamon sticks, cloves and lemon slice in a saucepan; heat to boiling. Simmer for 5 minutes. To serve, pour hot cider through a strainer into warm mugs. Add 1½ ounces rum to each cup. Float ½ teaspoon butter on each and garnish with a lemon twist. Serves 8.

COUNTRY INN APPLE SOUR

        1 ounce applejack
        1 ounce wild cherry brandy
    1½ ounces sweet cider
    1½ ounces sour drink mix
        Orange slice
        Maraschino cherry

Put all ingredients in a blender with crushed ice and blend. Pour into a goblet or snifter. Garnish with an orange slice and a maraschino cherry. Makes 1 drink.

Cheshire Inn & Lodge

St. Louis, Missouri

The style of Tudor country inns has been brought to life on the edge of St. Louis. The inn includes a pub, a baronial tavern and a restaurant as authentic as rare roast beef. Among the prides of the kitchen are Dover sole with almonds and pork chops Buckingham. A perfect accompaniment for the pork is Autumn Butternut Casserole, in which squash is transformed by the chef into a nutritious, pecan-topped side dish that is not difficult to prepare at home. It's also a great main dish for a meatless night at home.

AUTUMN BUTTERNUT CASSEROLE

   3 cups mashed, cooked butternut squash
   ¼ cup butter
   1 tablespoon brown sugar
   ¼ teaspoon salt
   Dash of white pepper
1½ tablespoons butter
   6 cups sliced unpared Jonathan apples
     (about 2 pounds)
   ¼ cup granulated sugar
1½ cups cornflakes, coarsely crushed
   ½ cup chopped pecans
   ½ cup brown sugar
   2 tablespoons melted butter

Season squash with ¼ cup butter, 1 tablespoon brown sugar, ¼ teaspoon salt, and pepper. Heat 1½ tablespoons butter in a skillet; add sliced apples, sprinkle with ¼ cup sugar, cover and simmer over low heat until barely tender (about 5 minutes). Spread in a 3-quart casserole; spoon mashed squash evenly over apples. Mix cornflakes with pecans, ½ cup brown sugar and melted butter. Sprinkle over squash. Bake in a 350° oven for 15 minutes. Makes 8 servings.

The White Gull Inn

Door County Fish Boil

The White Gull Inn

Fish Creek, Wisconsin

If the clambake is the Algonquin Indians' gift to New England, the outdoor fish boil is an equally festive tradition handed down by the Chippewas to rural cooks in Wisconsin and other parts of the Great Lakes region.
Up in Door County – sometimes called "the Cape Cod of the Midwest" – Andy Coulson's White Gull Inn is justly famous for its mouth-watering regional specialties like this hearty and festive meal.

At the White Gull, the hungry gather on Wednesdays, Fridays, Saturdays and Sundays for steaming plates of whitefish steaks and red potatoes boiled in cauldrons over an open fire.

Served glistening with butter, along with cole slaw, homestyle rye bread, and tart red cherry pie, the Door County Fish Boil is a tradition that can now fit into your eating plans in an easy at-home version you'll enjoy sharing with family and friends.

DOOR COUNTY FISH BOIL

12 small red potatoes
   Cheesecloth
 8 quarts water
 1 pound salt (2 cups)
12 1-inch-thick whitefish steaks or 1 fish,
   cut into steaks (2½ pounds)
   Melted butter
   Lemon wedges

Wash potatoes and cut a slice from each end. Tie potatoes in a cheesecloth bag. Put water in a large pot, preferably one with a removable basket or rack; bring to a boil. Add potatoes and half the salt; cook 20 minutes. Check doneness of potatoes; they should be almost done. Wrap fish in cheesecloth; add to pot with remaining salt. Cook 10 minutes. Skim fish oils from surface of water. Lift cooked potatoes and fish from cooking water; drain. Serve with melted butter and lemon. When cooking over an open fire, as it is done at the inn, the fish oils are boiled off by tossing a small amount of kerosene on the fire, causing the water to boil up and over. Makes 6 servings.

Old Rittenhouse Inn

Bayfield, Wisconsin

An impressive Victorian mansion built in 1890, the Old Rittenhouse is located near the shores of Lake Superior. Innkeepers Jerry and Mary Phillips have furnished their inn with antiques that bespeak Victorian style as elegantly as does the food. On a menu abounding with local specialties, perhaps most outstanding are the many fresh fruit attractions. Mary's Strawberry Consommé is a particularly refreshing first course with its fresh strawberries, rhubarb, and lacing of Burgundy wine and can easily be your specialty when summer fruits are on the market.

STRAWBERRY CONSOMMÉ

  1 pint fresh strawberries
1$\frac{2}{3}$ cups fresh or 16-ounce package frozen (thawed and drained) cut rhubarb
  1 3-inch stick cinnamon
$\frac{3}{4}$-1 cup sugar
  2 cups water (use juice from frozen rhubarb plus water)
  $\frac{1}{2}$ cup Burgundy wine
  $\frac{1}{2}$ cup soda water
    Sour cream

Set aside about 6 strawberries; cut up remainder; put in a saucepan with rhubarb, cinnamon stick, sugar and water. Bring to a boil, reduce heat, and simmer until rhubarb is tender, about 5 minutes. Pour into a strainer and press out juice. There should be 3 cups rosy-pink juice. Add Burgundy wine and soda. Slice remaining berries. Serve hot or chilled, garnished with sliced berries and dollops of sour cream. Makes 4-6 servings.

Jack Gleason's Fagleysville Country Hotel

Gilbertsville, Pennsylvania

In the heart of Schuylkill County, northwest of Philadelphia, this unpretentious crossroads red brick hotel attracts diners from far and wide. Its menu offers a variety of surprises such as beef with walnut-anchovy sauce, grilled onion wedges with a Korean dipping sauce, and trout stuffed Japanese style. As a delightful overture to this international style of dining, you will want to try Sweet-Sour Zucchini Salad with its hints of bacony goodness and the tang of red wine vinegar. It is a sure-to-please addition to your own repertoire.

SWEET-SOUR ZUCCHINI SALAD

2 strips bacon, chopped fine
1 tablespoon all-purpose flour
$1/3$ cup red wine vinegar
$2/3$ cup water
$1/4$ teaspoon pepper
$1/2$ teaspoon salt
2 tablespoons sugar
1 pound raw zucchini, shredded ($4\frac{1}{2}$ cups)
  Sliced tomatoes
  Sliced fresh mushrooms
  Salad greens

Cook bacon until crisp; remove from fat. In a saucepan, combine 1 tablespoon of the bacon fat with flour; cook slightly. Add vinegar, water, and seasonings. Cook and stir until thickened; add cooked bacon pieces. Cool. Just before serving, toss dressing with shredded zucchini. Arrange tomato and mushroom slices on salad greens. Top with a mound of zucchini mixture. Makes 6 servings.

Whaling Station Inn

Monterey, California

Tulip-shaped chandeliers and bentwood furniture are a decorative counterpoint to the Whaling Station's functional open hearth. Here, many of owner John Pesto's house specialties are broiled "just as the customer ordered." All are enhanced with the natural zest of wild herbs, which the owner gathers in the nearby Monterey hills. This Roasted Pacific Red Snapper, for instance, is memorable for its taste of wild thyme and fresh anise mingled delicately with Pernod and Cognac.

ROASTED PACIFIC RED SNAPPER

2 3-pound or 4 1½-pound red snappers, cleaned
   and scaled, heads on
8 small cloves garlic
¼ cup olive oil
1 teaspoon fresh or ½ teaspoon dried thyme
1½ cups fresh anise tops or fennel, if available, or
   1 tablespoon aniseed
2 cups fish or chicken broth
4 ounces Pernod
2 ounces Cognac

Trim fins from fish. Insert garlic into fish backs. Brush inside and outside of fish with olive oil; sprinkle with salt and pepper. Sprinkle outside of fish with thyme; fill fish cavities with fresh anise or aniseed. Place fish on an oiled rack in a roasting pan. Mix broth, Pernod, and Cognac; pour into pan under fish. Cover tightly with aluminum foil. Bake in a 475° oven for 15-25 minutes, depending on fish size. Remove foil and bake 10 minutes longer. Serve fish with pan juices and garnish with parsley. Makes 4-6 servings.

Lowell Inn

Stillwater, Minnesota

Three dining rooms generously furnished with antiques beckon Twin Cities visitors who come for lunch and dinner specialties reflecting Arthur Palmer's international tastes. The menu includes beef fondue, chicken livers with morels and barley-fed pork. The Lowell Inn's hot Red Cabbage is a superb accompaniment for pork and hearty sausage; its contrasting sweet and tart flavors appetizingly merge during a slow, gentle simmering.

RED CABBAGE

1 medium head red cabbage (2¾-3 pounds)
1 medium onion
2 large cooking apples (1 pound)
1 tablespoon bacon fat or butter
1½ cups water
1 cup cider vinegar
½ cup sugar
1 teaspoon salt
1 bay leaf
2 whole allspice
6 peppercorns
1 tablespoon cornstarch
2 tablespoons cold water

Wash cabbage and remove outer leaves; cut into quarters. Remove core and slice. (You should have about 3 quarts.) Slice onion. Pare apples and cut into sixths, removing core. Toss cabbage, onion and apples together in a Dutch oven. Add water, cider vinegar, sugar, salt and spices. Simmer, uncovered, 1 to 1½ hours, depending on degree of crispness desired. Combine cornstarch and cold water. Stir into hot cabbage; cook and stir until thickened, about 1 minute. Makes 8 servings.

The Elsah Landing

Elsah, Illinois

About thirty minutes from St. Louis, the Elsah
Landing offers no beds, but it is as pure a
country restaurant as you're likely to find.
The Landing's motto, "Soups, breads, and
desserts all made on the premises," attests to
its heartland spirit. But this spirit truly comes
alive with the fragrant aroma of loaves of
Cheddar Cheese Bread baking to golden-
brown doneness. Surprisingly easy to make at
home, this rich-tasting bread is especially
festive when baked in a coffee can to give it a
crisp-crusted "crown."

CHEDDAR CHEESE BREAD

      2 packages active dry yeast
      6 teaspoons sugar
      1 cup warm water (105° to 115°)
      ½ cup evaporated milk
      2 tablespoons soft shortening
      1 teaspoon salt
  4½-5 cups all-purpose flour
          1-pound package sharp Cheddar cheese-food
          spread (about 1¾ cups), at room temperature

Sprinkle yeast and 1 teaspoon sugar over ½ cup
warm water to soften. In large mixer bowl, combine milk, remaining water and sugar, shorten-
ing, salt and 1 cup flour. Beat at slow speed until
well mixed. Beat in yeast mixture and cheese
spread; beat in 2 cups flour. Remove from
mixer and stir in 1½ cups flour. Turn dough out
onto a floured surface and knead until smooth
and elastic, adding flour as needed. Grease a
large mixing bowl; turn dough in bowl to grease
top. Cover and let rise in a warm place for 2
hours. Punch down and shape into 2 loaves.
Place in 2 greased 8½x4½x2½-inch bread pans
or 2 greased 2-lb. coffee cans. Let rise in a warm
place 1 hour and 15 minutes. Bake in a 375°
oven for 35 minutes. Makes 2 loaves.

Boder's on the River

Mequon, Wisconsin

A stone's throw north of Milwaukee, Boder's offers the best of cooking based on Wisconsin's native foods. The crisp-roasted ducks served with wild rice are locally raised, whitefish is fresh from Lake Superior, and milk-fed veal has made both Boder's and Wisconsin famous. Rich with local farm products, the regionally famous Zwiebelkuchen was popular long before quiches were in vogue. This onion pie may be served as a finger appetizer or as a refreshing luncheon entrée accompanied by fresh fruit.

ZWIEBELKUCHEN (Onion Pie)

1 cup all-purpose flour
¼ teaspoon salt
   Dash sugar
½ cup butter, at room temperature
2 tablespoons milk
6 slices bacon, cut into small pieces
3 cups chopped onions
2 eggs, beaten
1 egg yolk, beaten
¾ cup sour cream
½ teaspoon salt
⅛ teaspoon pepper
1 teaspoon chopped chives
¼ teaspoon caraway seeds

Sift flour, ¼ teaspoon salt and sugar into bowl. Cut in butter. Add milk, mixing with a fork to moisten flour. Shape into a ball; wrap and chill 1 hour. Roll out between wax paper to fit a 9-inch pie plate. Prick lightly. Bake in a 350° oven for 10 minutes, until lightly brown. Cool. Fry bacon until crisp; remove from fat. Sauté onion in fat until soft. Drain onion. Combine remaining ingredients, except caraway seeds, beating lightly; add onion. Pour into baked crust; sprinkle with seeds. Bake in a 375° oven 30-35 minutes. Cut into 36-40 bite size pieces or 6-8 wedges.

the 1770 House

Tomatoes Country Style

the 1770 House

East Hampton, New York

On Main Street, in this summer retreat
for Manhattanities, Miriam and Sid Perle
converted a charming colonial house into an
inn crowded with antiques, but visitors are
chiefly attracted by the exceptional dinners
created in the modern kitchen.

Miriam Perle has described her cooking style
as "haute American," a term drawn from
her years as mistress of her own cooking
school. She adapts recipes to the foods locally
available on Long Island's southern shore.
She may serve swordfish al pesto, sea trout
with lemon herb sauce, sole steamed in
the Chinese manner, or Long Island duck
glazed with ginger.

Among the meal accompaniments is this
exceptional dish, Tomatoes Country Style.
In it, slices of Long Island beefsteak tomatoes
combined with a zesty cheese filling
are breaded and crisply fried. It makes a
superb vegetable course and one easily
recreated in your kitchen.

TOMATOES COUNTRY STYLE

1 clove garlic, minced
¼ cup minced parsley
⅛ teaspoon salt
  8-ounce package cream cheese, softened
1 teaspoon chopped fresh or ½ teaspoon dried basil
  leaves, optional
4 beefsteak or other large tomatoes
½ cup all-purpose flour
1 egg, beaten with 1 tablespoon milk
⅔ cup dry bread crumbs
3 tablespoons butter
3 tablespoons olive oil
  Fresh basil or parsley, optional

Beat together in mixer, or process in food processor, the garlic, parsley, salt and cream cheese;
add basil, if desired. Cut tomatoes into 12 even
slices, about ½ inch thick. Spread 6 slices with
about 2 tablespoons of cream cheese mixture
each; top with remaining slices to make 6 sandwiches. Dip each in flour, then in egg mixture,
and finally in crumbs. Fry on both sides over
medium heat in mixture of butter and olive oil
until brown. Garnish with fresh basil or parsley,
if desired. Makes 6 servings.

Arizona Inn

Tucson, Arizona

Since Isabella Gardner first established her sanctuary for Southwestern arts outside Tucson, the Arizona Inn has added lodging and dining for discriminating guests. Now run by her son John, the inn specializes in such sunbelt favorites as eggplant with medallions of beef and artichoke hearts. A perfect luncheon dish is this unusual combination of seafood and fruit called Arizona Inn Salad, often served beside the pool.

ARIZONA INN SALAD

2 14-ounce packages frozen cooked, peeled and
   deveined shrimp (3 cups)
1 cup finely chopped celery
3 hard-cooked eggs, chopped
½ cup mayonnaise
2 teaspoons curry powder
   Salt and pepper
3 small or 1½ large ripe cantaloupe, chilled
   Salad greens
   Asparagus spears
   Strawberries
   Bunches of green grapes
   Hard-cooked egg wedges
   Lemon wedges
   Celery leaves

Defrost shrimp. Combine with chopped celery and eggs. Combine mayonnaise and curry powder; season to taste with salt and pepper. Toss with shrimp mixture. To serve, cut cantaloupe in halves or quarters, depending on size; remove seeds. Arrange salad greens and melons on individual plates. Fill melon sections with shrimp salad. Garnish with asparagus spears, fruit, egg wedges, lemon wedges and celery leaves. Makes 6 main-dish salads.

Rancho Encantado

Sour Cream Chicken Enchiladas

Rancho Encantado

Santa Fe, New Mexico

The "enchanted ranch," as this Spanish name is translated, has grown from a small adobe country hotel to a contemporary stop-off in chaparral country where guests are afforded the double pleasure of partaking of fine dining and the beautiful desert scenery.

Entrées range from butterflied pork chops cooked in beer to steak marinated with local chili peppers. "The dish we are best known for is the Sour Cream Chicken Enchilada," says innkeeper John Egan, adding that the enchilada was the creation of early Spanish settlers who lived in New Mexico, southern Colorado and Arizona.

John Egan recommends the Rancho's recipe for their popular enchiladas as the focal point of your next patio party. Radiant with contrasting tastes and textures, they are especially festive when topped with sour cream and guacamole, and served with a curry-pineapple-flavored shrimp appetizer and a custardy dessert called flan.

SOUR CREAM CHICKEN ENCHILADAS

2 cups cut-up cooked chicken (½-inch pieces)
1 cup sour cream
⅛ teaspoon salt
   Dash pepper
12 5-inch corn tortillas
   Cooking oil
   4-ounce can chopped green chilies, drained, or
   10-ounce can green or red enchilada sauce
2 cups shredded white Cheddar or Monterey Jack
   cheese
   Shredded lettuce
   Cherry tomatoes, halved, or chopped tomatoes
½-¾ cup sour cream and/or guacamole
   Tortilla chips

Combine chicken, sour cream, salt and pepper. Quickly fry 1 tortilla at a time in hot oil (375°) to soften. Spoon a heaping tablespoon of chicken mixture onto each, spread down center and roll. Place, seam side down, in an oiled 13x9x2-inch baking dish. When all tortillas are filled and rolled, spoon over either green chilies or enchilada sauce; top with cheese. Bake in a 400° oven for 12 to 15 minutes or until cheese is melted and enchiladas are hot.

To serve, put 2 or 3 enchiladas on a serving plate; surround with shredded lettuce and to-matoes. Top with sour cream, guacamole, or both; stand tortilla chips in sour cream or guacamole. Makes 4-6 servings.

Sword Gate Inn

Charleston, South Carolina

The surrounding countryside was still marshy when the earliest rooms of the inn were built, and the stately architecture suggests the colonial beginnings of this intimate house where breakfast is a culinary celebration. Lodgers are treated to hominy grits and sizzling bacon along with such classics as these very special Sword Gate Cinnamon Breakfast Apples. Prepared in minutes, they make a surprising and rewarding way to "break fast" at your home, when slathered generously on buttered hot biscuits or breads.

CINNAMON BREAKFAST APPLES

1 cup sugar
1 teaspoon cinnamon
¼ teaspoon nutmeg
4 or 5 large cooking apples (about 1½ pounds)
2 tablespoons water
¼ cup butter

Combine sugar, cinnamon and nutmeg. Pare apples and chop into bite-size pieces. Put in a 4-cup measure, sprinkling with cinnamon sugar as you add apples. When you have 4 cups, put apples, water and butter into a sauce-pan. Cover and cook over low to medium heat, stirring once or twice, for 15-20 minutes or until apples are tender. Serve for breakfast with biscuits or grits and eggs. Makes 2⅔ cups.

The Wine Country Inn

Strawberry Nut Bread

The Wine Country Inn

St. Helena, California

As if it had been a Napa Valley landmark for decades, the rosy-roofed inn where Ned and Marge Smith preside was designed in 1975 to look as well-aged as vintage wine. The mansard tower of local stone is buttressed by board-and-batten walls, and inside, the inn is dominated by a spacious common room for lodgers.

Aiming at a "bed and breakfast" theme, the Smiths didn't open the inn until there were enough good restaurants serving dinner in the valley. On the long common room harvest table is a collection of menus from places they recommend for dining.

On the same table they serve splendid morning repasts with three or four juices, four or five fresh fruits, hot coffee, herb teas and their own homemade breads, like this Strawberry Nut Bread. Its aroma alone would make a sensational call to breakfast for any treasured house guest.

STRAWBERRY NUT BREAD

2 10-ounce packages frozen sliced strawberries
4 eggs
1 cup cooking oil
2 cups sugar
3 cups all-purpose flour
1 tablespoon cinnamon
1 teaspoon baking soda
1 teaspoon salt
1¼ cups chopped nuts

Defrost strawberries. Beat eggs in a bowl until fluffy; add cooking oil, sugar and defrosted strawberries. Sift together flour, cinnamon, soda and salt into a mixing bowl; add strawberry mixture and mix until well blended. Stir in nuts. Pour into 2 greased and floured 9½x5x3-inch or 8½x4½x2½-inch loaf pans. Bake in a 350° oven for 1 hour and 10 minutes or until done. Cool in pans for 10 minutes, then turn out of pans and cool on racks. Makes 2 loaves. This bread slices best when chilled. May be sliced and warmed to serve with butter for breakfast or brunch or sliced thinly, spread with whipped cream cheese and served with fruit salad for lunch or used to make tea sandwiches.

La Provence

Lacombe, Louisiana

Surrounded by legendary restaurants, many New Orleanians consider La Provence (just across Lake Pontchartrain) superlative. Reminiscent of a fine French country inn, the menu includes such delicacies as chef Chris Keras' duckling bigarade, broiled marinated quail and sautéed julienne of leeks. A masterpiece from this classic repertoire is the chef's savory Gambas aux Petites Légumes. This unusual recipe for a cooked shrimp appetizer is redolent with the taste of fennel and Ricard or Pernod.

GAMBAS AUX PETITES LÉGUMES

1 cup each diced carrot, onion and celery
$^1/_3$ cup diced fresh fennel or 1 teaspoon fennel seeds
2 tablespoons butter
2 tablespoons olive oil
1 pound peeled and deveined shrimp (26-30)
1 tablespoon minced shallots
1 tablespoon Ricard or Pernod
1 cup fresh cream
1 tablespoon lime juice
¼ teaspoon salt
   Dash white pepper
   Fresh fennel leaves

Quickly blanch vegetables in boiling salted water; drain and chill in ice water. Heat butter and olive oil in a frypan over high heat; add shrimp and shallots; sauté quickly, stirring constantly. Remove from heat; pour Ricard or Pernod over and flame. When flame dies, remove shrimp and keep warm. Add cream, lime juice and seasoning to pan juices; boil to reduce about one-third. Add shrimp and half the drained vegetables. Heat but do not boil. Spoon into individual dishes. Garnish with remaining vegetables and fresh fennel leaves. Makes 4 servings.

The Golden Lamb

Braised Lamb Shanks

The Golden Lamb

Lebanon, Ohio

An easy trip from Cincinnati, The Golden Lamb
was originally built as a log cabin in 1803.
From this humble beginning, the inn rightly
points with pride to the fact it has played host
to ten U.S. presidents as well as literary
notables like Mark Twain and Charles Dickens.

While the frontier architecture has long
since been transformed by four-story brick
walls, The Golden Lamb is an embracing
monument to nineteenth-century innkeeping.

The food is equally reflective of a splendid
past. Salt-cured ham steaks are saucy with
bourbon glaze; chicken in cream is served on
sour-cream corn bread.

Braised Lamb Shanks are famous for their
combination of flavors that evoke memories
of an almost forgotten culinary era. Simmered
gently with mushrooms, celery and turnips,
they are so tender the meat barely clings
to the bones.

BRAISED LAMB SHANKS

4-6 lamb shanks (about 4-6 pounds)
  ¼ teaspoon black pepper
  1 teaspoon salt
  3 tablespoons fat
  1 cup diced onion
  1 cup quartered mushrooms (about ¼ pound)
  ¾ cup sliced celery
  1 cup diced turnips
  ⅓ cup all-purpose flour
  3 tablespoons tomato paste
  ¼ teaspoon finely chopped fresh or ⅛ teaspoon
    crushed dried rosemary
  ¼ teaspoon fresh or ⅛ teaspoon dried thyme leaves
  1 large bay leaf
  2 cloves garlic, minced
  ½ cup Burgundy wine
  3 cups lamb or beef stock

Season lamb shanks with salt and pepper. Heat fat in a large Dutch oven or heavy roaster. Brown lamb shanks on all sides in hot fat; remove from pan. Add onion, mushrooms, celery and turnips to pan; cook and stir till brown. Add flour, stirring to brown lightly. Stir in tomato paste, seasonings, wine and stock. Return lamb shanks to pan; bring to a boil. Cover and bake in a 350° oven for 2 hours or until tender. Remove lamb shanks to a hot platter and keep warm. Skim fat from sauce. Spoon over lamb shanks. Makes 4-6 servings.

The Bishop's Lodge

Santa Fe, New Mexico

Five minutes from Santa Fe in the Sangre de Cristo foothills, the lodge accommodates several dozen guests and has spacious dining rooms glinting with Southwestern ambiance. The restaurant is known for barbecued beef, fresh mountain fish, butterflied lamb with mountain herbs, and Spanish specialties. A lodge favorite is this chicken-based Cream of Almond Soup that makes a subtle foil for the more substantial courses that follow.

CREAM OF ALMOND SOUP

 3 tablespoons almond paste (1½ ounces)
⅔ cup finely chopped almonds
 2 quarts chicken broth
 3 egg yolks, slightly beaten
 2 cups whipping cream
½ teaspoon sugar
½ teaspoon salt
¼ teaspoon almond extract

Add almond paste and chopped almonds to chicken broth; cover and bring to a boil. Lower heat and simmer for 30 minutes. Beat together egg yolks, cream, sugar and salt. Beat a small amount of hot broth into egg mixture, then add to remaining hot broth, beating with a wire whisk. Cook over low heat until mixture thickens slightly, whisking constantly. Do not boil. Add almond extract. May be served hot or chilled. Top with sliced almonds, if desired. Makes 8 servings.

104

San Ysidro Ranch

Carré d'Agneau Dijonnais

San Ysidro Ranch

Montecito, California

Ronald Coleman, 1940s Hollywood star, once owned San Ysidro, and for years it has been a hideout for pleasure seekers from Los Angeles and Santa Barbara. A couple of centuries earlier, the ranch was one of California's string of early Franciscan missions, and the building used at a later time by the padres as a fruit-packing house is now a candlelit restaurant.

Innkeeper Jim Lavenson, who once ran New York's Plaza Hotel, offers his guests many delights, including an "honor bar" where guests help themselves to cocktails or, in the morning, to juice freshly squeezed from ranch-grown oranges. The menu nods to the Spanish past with Red Snapper Vera Cruz, but it is also rich with continental specialties like the classic lamb roast known as Carré d'Agneau Dijonnais.

Delicately painted with aromatic Dijon mustard, this rack of lamb is most succulent when served medium rare. Hot herbed tomato halves or artichoke bottoms stuffed with lemon-accented mushroom purée are simple, yet elegant, accompaniments.

CARRÉ D'AGNEAU DIJONNAIS

3 8-bone racks of lamb
  Flour to dredge
½ cup clarified butter
6 tablespoons Dijon mustard
2 cups coarse bread crumbs
2 tablespoons chopped parsley
2 teaspoons each chopped fresh or ½ teaspoon each
  dried oregano and basil
2 teaspoons grated parmesan cheese
2 teaspoons minced garlic
1 teaspoon minced shallots

Have butcher remove meat from bones and
sinew. Trim off fell and fat. Sprinkle both sides
of lamb with salt and pepper; dredge in flour.
Brown on all sides in clarified butter over
moderate-to-high heat. Remove from pan and
pat dry. Combine shallots, garlic, cheese, basil,
oregano and salt and pepper to taste with
bread crumbs; mix well. Coat lamb liberally
with mustard; roll in seasoned bread crumbs,
patting firmly so bread crumbs stick. Place
on a greased broiler rack or in buttered pan.
Moisten bread crumb mixture with butter and
cook in a 425° oven for approximately 15-18
minutes, or until firm but resilient to touch
(medium rare). Makes 6 servings.

Historical Briarhurst Manor Inn

Manitou Springs, Colorado

When dining at this stately mansion, the breathtaking Rocky Mountains scenery is an experience rivaled only by the Continental cuisine of chef Sigi Krauss. There is a champagne brunch on Sundays, and lunch and dinner throughout the week. Here is chef Sigi's high-altitude version of the internationally famous Fondue Neufchâtel, a Swiss dip-in dish with which you can delight friends at a casual dinner.

FONDUE NEUFCHÂTEL

1 small clove garlic, cut in half
2 cups California dry white wine
8 ounces Swiss Emmentaler cheese, shredded (2 cups)
8 ounces Swiss Gruyère cheese, shredded (2 cups)
4 ounces cooked smoked ham, diced (1 cup)
1 ounce kirsch liqueur (2 tablespoons)
¾ teaspoon cornstarch
⅛ teaspoon salt
⅛ teaspoon white pepper
　Dash nutmeg
　Dash cloves
4 scallions, chopped
　Crusty French bread, cut into 1-inch cubes

Rub sides of a 2-quart earthenware fondue pot with cut garlic. Pour in wine and heat over high heat to a boil. Add cheeses, a scant cupful at a time, stirring to melt after each addition. When all cheese is added continue to cook and stir until mixture is smooth and thickened. Add ham. Mix kirsch with cornstarch; stir into hot cheese mixture. Season. Sprinkle scallions over. Serve with crusty bread cubes. Makes 4 servings.

Welshfield Inn

Poppy Seed Dressing

Welshfield Inn

Burton, Ohio

On U.S. 422 between Cleveland and
Youngstown, the Welshfield Inn has been a
landmark for 150 years, its authenticity
apparent in its white-columned front.
Surrounded by picturesque Amish farm
country, the inn draws travelers hungry for
the kinds of "from-scratch" meals that
deserve to be praised as generous,
wholesome and tasty.

Here, skillet-fried chicken is, as the menu
boasts, "the way grandmother used to make
it." Fresh fruits of the season, oozing their own
sun-sweet juices, are served as salads,
appetizers, or even desserts.

A crowning glory for your fruit salads is the
Welshfield Inn's noteworthy Poppy Seed
Dressing. The sweet and tart zest and gentle
bite of this dressing contrasts the fruits' subtle
flavors without overpowering them.

POPPY SEED DRESSING

  1 cup sugar or honey
1¼ teaspoons salt
  ½ cup vinegar
1⅓ cups salad oil (vegetable oil)
  1 tablespoon grated onion
1¼ teaspoons dry mustard
  2 teaspoons poppy seeds

Combine sugar, salt and vinegar in a sauce pan; heat over low heat until sugar dissolves. If using honey, skip preceding step. Pour dissolved sugar into a quart jar; add salad oil, onion, mustard and poppy seeds; shake to mix. Refrigerate. Shake before serving. Makes about 2½ cups. Spoon over salad of fresh fruits in season (summer — peaches, plums, strawberries, melons; winter — grapefruit, oranges, apples, avocado).

Miner's Delight Inn

Lander, Wyoming

"A miner's delight" once was a gold rush phrase for something more than a flash in the pan. Its meaning now has even better connotations for gourmets. Paul and Georgina Newman have created a restaurant with the highest gastronomic standards in the Rockies. Memories of the Forty-Niners, who carried their own sourdough starter to make flapjacks, are conjured up by a dish named Manicotti Miner's Delight. This pancake creation is one your family is bound to cheer for, especially when you team up a meat-filled and a cheese-filled pancake.

MANICOTTI MINER'S DELIGHT

1 recipe Pancakes (See below)
1 recipe each Meat and Cheese Fillings (See below)
1 16-ounce jar spaghetti sauce with mushrooms
1 cup shredded mozzarella or Swiss cheese

Pancakes: Beat 6 eggs, 1 cup milk, 1½ cups all-purpose flour and ½ teaspoon salt together. Bake on a lightly greased, moderately hot crêpe pan on one side only. Makes 16.

Meat Filling: Cook 2 cups chopped onion and 1 minced clove garlic in 1 tablespoon olive oil; add ½-lb. chopped mushrooms; remove from heat. Stir in 1½-lbs. ground beef, 1½ cups diced mozzarella or Swiss cheese, 1 cup soft bread crumbs, 1 egg, 1½ teaspoons salt, and ¼ teaspoon each oregano and pepper.

Cheese Filling: Combine 1½ cups Ricotta cheese, ½ cup grated Romano cheese, ¼ cup chopped parsley, 2 eggs, 1½ teaspoons salt and ⅛ teaspoon pepper.

Spoon Meat Filling on 8 pancakes; Cheese Filling on remainder. Roll and place seam side down in a greased 13x9x2-inch baking dish. Spoon spaghetti sauce over; sprinkle with cheese. Bake in a 350° oven for 30-40 minutes. Makes 8 servings.

116

Salishan Lodge

Fillet of Sole Marguery

Salishan Lodge

Gleneden Beach, Oregon

A haven for lovers of the coastal lands of
Oregon, Salishan Lodge was built by a
Portland manufacturer who wanted to share
with others the beauties he enjoyed as an
outdoorsman.

The outdoors is wrapped around the clear
glass walls of the split-level dining room
where the Continental-American cuisine of
chef Franz Buck is served. There are Roquefort crêpes flavored with Metaxa, plank-broiled
Chinook salmon from adjacent Pacific streams,
Dungeness crabs and tiny Oregon oysters.

One of the most widely recognized
specialties, Fillet of Sole Marguery, is the
Salishan variation on a classic theme. While
the lodge uses native West Coast Petrale
sole, you can prepare this entrée superbly
with the freshest sole in your market. It is a
dish to make friends lift one more glass in
salute to your stylish cooking.

FILLET OF SOLE MARGUERY

4 Petrale or other sole fillets (about 1-1½ pounds)
4 teaspoons minced shallots
½ pound mushrooms, sliced (2½ cups)
1 cup peeled and deveined small shrimp (6 ounces)
¼ cup fish stock or chicken broth
¼ cup Sauterne
1 cup Hollandaise Sauce (See below)

Fold fillets in half crosswise. In a buttered fry-pan, sprinkle shallots; arrange fillets atop. Sprinkle fish with salt and pepper. Fit mushrooms and shrimp around fish. Combine fish stock and Sauterne; pour over fillets. Bring to a boil; reduce heat, cover and simmer 6-8 minutes. Place fillets onto a heated platter. Arrange mushrooms and shrimp atop fish; keep warm. Boil fish stock and wine; reduce to about 6 tablespoons. Strain and fold into Hollandaise Sauce; pour sauce over fish. Makes 4 servings.

Hollandaise Sauce: Combine 2 egg yolks, 1 tablespoon lemon juice and 1 tablespoon warm water in the top of a double boiler. Bring water in bottom of double boiler to a slow boil. Put top over water and whisk rapidly until mixture doubles in volume. Add 11 tablespoons soft butter, one at a time, whisking rapidly as you add. When all butter is added, remove from hot water. Season with salt, white pepper and monosodium glutamate. Makes 1 cup.

SALISHAN LODGE

The Inn at Rancho Santa Fe

Rancho Santa Fe, California

They say Mary Pickford used to steal away from Hollywood for the peace and quiet of the Inn at Rancho Santa Fe. A few miles north of San Diego, it is nestled amid an oasis of bougainvillea, palm trees, magnolias and strawberry trees. The inn offers superb dining with specialties such as Boneless Breast of Chicken Saltimbocca, which combines the delicacy of chicken breasts with Monterey Jack cheese and the piquancy of prosciutto, spices and sherry.

BONELESS BREAST OF CHICKEN SALTIMBOCCA

6 whole boneless, skinned chicken breasts, cut in half
⅓ cup plus 1 tablespoon all-purpose flour
⅓ cup clarified butter
12 thin slices prosciutto ham
6 1-ounce slices Monterey Jack cheese, cut in half
¼ cup chopped shallots
3 large cloves garlic, minced
½ pound mushrooms, sliced (about 3 cups)
½ cup dry white wine
1 cup chicken broth
1 teaspoon each fresh thyme and oregano or
  ½ teaspoon each dried thyme and oregano leaves
½ cup each dry sherry and cream
  Salt and pepper

Dip chicken in flour; brown in butter. Arrange in a buttered 13x9x2-inch baking dish. Top each with 1 slice prosciutto ham and ½ slice cheese. Cook shallots and garlic until soft; add mushrooms, wine, broth and herbs. Bring to a boil, and cook 10 minutes. Stir into hot mixture 1 tablespoon flour and a small amount of sherry. Stir in remaining sherry and cream; season with salt and pepper. Pour sauce over chicken. Bake in a 375° oven for 20 minutes. Makes 6 servings.

The Captain Whidbey Inn

Washington Apple Cake

The Captain Whidbey Inn

Coupeville, Washington

Ninety minutes from Seattle, this wilderness
lodge on Whidbey Island attracts weekenders
seeking peace and quiet as well as salmon
fishermen and seafood lovers.

The Stone family, in residence since 1964,
has preserved the remoteness of the inn's
location (no TV, no telephones), but brought
the world to the Whidbey kitchen. Here Shirley
Stone supervises menus that deal sophisti-
catedly with salmon, Dungeness crab and
Olympia oysters, in addition to "land foods"
like roast beef, tenderly ministered steaks and
succulent baby lamb.

The perfect ending to a meal at the Captain
Whidbey is the inn's Washington Apple Cake.
This dessert, originated close to home, is
aromatic with spices and the fragrance of
Washington state orchards, and offers a fitting
climax to a meal served amid the tranquility
of nature.

WASHINGTON APPLE CAKE

3 eggs
2 cups sugar
1 cup cooking oil
2 cups all-purpose flour
2 teaspoons cinnamon
1 teaspoon baking soda
½ teaspoon salt
1 teaspoon vanilla
1 cup chopped walnuts
4 cups thinly sliced pared tart apples (5 medium)

Beat eggs with a mixer until thick and light. Combine sugar and oil; pour into eggs with mixer on medium speed. Stir together flour, cinnamon, soda and salt; add to egg mixture with vanilla; beat to mix. Stir in walnuts. Spread apples in a buttered 13x9x2-inch pan. Pour batter over apples, spreading to cover. Bake in a 350° oven for 1 hour. Remove from oven and cool. Spread with Cream Cheese Icing.

Cream Cheese Icing: Soften 2 3-ounce packages cream cheese. Beat until fluffy. Beat in ¼ cup melted butter; then beat in 2 cups powdered sugar and 1 teaspoon lemon juice. Spread over cooled cake. Refrigerate. Makes 12-15 servings.

INN INDEX

ARIZONA

Grand Canyon. El Tovar Lodge. Grand Canyon National Park Lodges 86023; (602) 638-2631. From Flagstaff, take U.S. 180 to Rte. 64 and go north 23 mi. to south entrance of Grand Canyon Village — El Tovar is about 4½ mi. Cantaloupe Mousse, page 40.

Tucson. Arizona Inn. 2200 East Elm Street 85719; (602) 325-1541. From Phoenix take I-10 south to Speedway Blvd. then east to University of Arizona, turn left on Campbell, 5 blocks to East Elm. Arizona Inn Salad, page 86.

CALIFORNIA

Columbia. City Hotel. Main Street, P.O. Box 1870, 95310; (209) 532-1479. From Stockton take I-5 to Manteca, then follow Rte. 120 east to Rte. 108 which will take you to Sonora. Take Rte. 49 north 2½ mi., then 2 mi. on Parrots Ferry Road to Columbia. Fettine de Vitello Piccata, page 32.

Montecito. San Ysidro Ranch. 900 San Ysidro Lane 93108; (805) 969-5046. From Santa Barbara take Rte. 101 south to Montecito, then go north on San Ysidro Road through Montecito Village to San Ysidro Lane. Carré d'Agneau Dijonnais, page 108.

Monterey. Whaling Station Inn. 763 Wave Street 93940; (408) 373-4248. One block above Cannery Row in Monterey. Roasted Pacific Red Snapper, page 76.

Rancho Santa Fe. The Inn at Rancho Santa Fe. P.O. Box 869, 92014; (714) 756-1131. From Los Angeles take I-5 to Encinitas Blvd. or Lomas Santa Fe exits; from San Diego take I-5 north to Via De La Valle exit — about 5 mi. to Paseo Delicias, main street of Rancho Santa Fe. Boneless Breast of Chicken Saltimbocca, page 122.

St. Helena. The Wine Country Inn. 1152 Lodi Lane 95474; (707) 963-7077. From San Francisco cross Oakland Bay Bridge to Rte. 80, then go north to Napa cutoff. Follow Rte. 29 through St. Helena to Lodi Lane, about 2 mi. north; turn east ¼ mi. to inn. Strawberry Nut Bread, page 96.

COLORADO

Manitou Springs. Historical Briarhurst Manor Inn. 404 Manitou Ave. 80829; (303) 685-5828. From Denver take I-25 south to Colorado Springs, then follow U.S. 24 west to Manitou Springs; exit at Manitou Ave. Inn is next to Buffalo Bill Wax Museum. Fondue Neufchâtel, page 110.

CONNECTICUT

Essex. Griswold Inn. Main Street 06426; (203) 767-0991. From I-95 take Exit 69, go north on Rte. 9 to Exit 3. Turn right at stop light and follow West Ave. to town center; turn right onto Main St. Veal Birds Griswold and Cheddar Cheese Grits Soufflés, page 10.

Ridgefield. Stonehenge. 06877; (203) 438-6511. Take U.S. 7 to Ridgefield. Stonehenge Chocolate Whiskey Cake, page 33.

FLORIDA

Captiva Island. Chadwick's Restaurant South Seas Plantation 33924; (813) 472-3141. From Fort Myers take Rte. 867 over toll bridge and causeway to Sanibel thence to Captiva Island. Puff 'N' Stuff Balls, page 36.

Lake Wales. Chalet Suzanne Restaurant & Inn. 1 Chalet Suzanne Drive, Box AC, 33853; (813) 676-1477. From Tampa follow I-4 east to Rte. 27, then turn south to inn 4 mi. north of Lake Wales. Roquefort Mousse Dean, page 54.

ILLINOIS

Elsah. The Elsah Landing. 18 LaSalle Street 62028; (618) 374-1607. Take Rte. 270 from St. Louis to Rte. 367 thence north to Alton, Illinois; follow River Road 12 mi. to Elsah. Cheddar Cheese Bread, page 79.

INDIANA

Batesville. Sherman House. 35 South Main Street 47006; (812) 934-2407. From Cincinnati or Indianapolis take I-74 to Rte. 229 then south to inn. Beef Wellington, page 39.

KENTUCKY

Berea. Boone Tavern Hotel and Dining Room. Berea College 40403; (606) 986-9341 ext. 200. From Lexington take I-75 south to U.S. 25; Boone Tavern is in center of Berea, across from campus. Spiced Cranberry Rolls, page 14.

Harrodsburg. Beaumont Inn. 638 Beaumont Drive 40330; (606) 734-3381. From Louisville take I-64 east to Exit 48, then go south on Rte. 151 to U.S. 127, continuing south to Harrodsburg. Cream of Broccoli Soup, page 64.

LOUISIANA

Lacombe. La Provence. P.O. Box 805, 70445; (504) 626-7662. From New Orleans take causeway across Lake Ponchartrain; turn right on Rte. 190 7½ mi. to La Provence, on Mandeville-Slidell Road. Gambas aux Petites Légumes, page 98.

MAINE

Wiscasset. Squire Tarbox Inn. Westport Island, RFD 2, Box 318, 04578; (207) 882-7693. From Maine Turnpike take Exit 9 and follow I-95 and U.S. 1 to Rte. 144, 8 mi. north of Bath. Follow 144 to Wiscasset-Westport Bridge, then 6 mi. south to inn. Blueberry Gingerbread, page 30.

MARYLAND

Oxford. Robert Morris Inn. 21654; (301) 226-5111. From Delaware Memorial Bridge follow Rte. 13 south to Rte. 301 then go south to Rte. 50, then east to Easton. From Chesapeake Bay Bridge follow Rte. 50-301 to Rte. 50 and go east to Easton. From Chesapeake Bay Tunnel take Rte. 13 north to Rte. 50 and go west to Easton. From Easton follow Rte. 322 to Rte. 333 to Oxford. Oysters à la Gino, page 44.

MASSACHUSETTS

Nantucket Island. Jared Coffin House. Broad Street 02554; (617) 288-2400. Year-round ferry from Woods Hole, MA, mid-June – mid-September and January – March. From Hyannis, MA, April – December; car reservations – Phone (617) 540-2022. Scallops Sautéed with Herbs and Vegetables, page 4.

Sturbridge. Publick House. On the Common 01566; (617) 347-3313. Take I-86 to Sturbridge exit, Mass. Turnpike to Exit 9, inn is on Rte. 131. New England Clam Chowder, page 6.

Sudbury. Longfellow's Wayside Inn. 01776; (617) 443-8848. From New York take I-90 to U.S. 495, turning north to Rte. 20, then 7 mi. east to inn. From Boston take I-90 to Rte. 128 Weston exit, then north on Rte. 128 to Exit 49, then go west 11 mi. on Rte. 20. Yankee Pot Roast, page 46.

MINNESOTA

New Prague. Schumacher's New Prague Hotel. 212 West Main St. 56071; (612) 758-2133. From Minneapolis take U.S. 494 west to U.S. 169; go south to Jordan exit and take Rte. 21 9 mi. to New Prague. At stop sign turn left to Main – inn is in second block on the right. Escargots à la Nancy, page 60.

Stillwater. Lowell Inn. 102 N. Second St. 55082; (612) 439-1100. From St. Paul take Rte. 36 east to Stillwater's Main St., turn left at second light, go 1 block to inn on corner. Red Cabbage, page 78.

MISSISSIPPI

Pascagoula. Longfellow House. 3401 East Beach 39567; (601) 762-1122. Take U.S. 90 from Mobile or Gulfport to Pascagoula; turn south on Market St. to Beach Blvd. and turn left. Sweet Edna Lou, page 35.

MISSOURI

St. Louis. Cheshire Inn & Lodge. 6300 Clayton Road 63117; (314) 647-7300. Follow Clayton Road west to Skinker. Autumn Butternut Casserole, page 68.

NEW HAMPSHIRE

Lyme. The Lyme Inn. On the Common 03768; (603) 795-2222. Take I-91 north to East Thetford exit, cross Connecticut River to Lyme. Hasenpfeffer, page 37.

NEW MEXICO

Santa Fe. The Bishop's Lodge. P.O. Box 2367, 87501; (505) 983-6377. From Santa Fe take Bishop's Lodge Road north 3 mi. to inn, sign on right. Cream of Almond Soup, page 104.

Santa Fe. Rancho Encantado. Rte. 4, Box 57C, 87501; (505) 982-3537. Take Rte. 285 north from Santa Fe to Tesuque exit, then follow road roughly 3 mi. You will find Rte. 22 on right, with sign indicating "Rancho Encantado 2 mi. on right." Sour Cream Chicken Enchiladas, page 90.

NEW YORK

Dover Plains. Old Drovers Inn. 12522; (914) 832-9311. Follow Rte. 22 for 2 mi. north of Pawling, NY to Duncan Hill Road East. Browned Turkey Hash with Mustard Sauce, page 55.

East Hampton. the 1770 House. 143 Main Street 11937; (516) 324-1770. Take Long Island Expressway to Exit 70, then turn south to Rte. 27 East, onto Main St.; inn is diagonally across from Guild Hall. Tomatoes Country Style, page 84.

Garrison. The Bird & Bottle Inn. 10524; (914) 424-3000. From George Washington Bridge follow Palisades Pkwy. north to Bear Mtn. Bridge; cross bridge and go north on Rte. 9D 4½ mi. to Rte. 403. Proceed on Rte. 403 to Rte. 9, then north 4 mi. From I-84 take Exit 13 and follow Rte. 9 south 8 mi. Black Bean Soup, page 52.

Hillsdale. L'Hostellerie Bressane. P.O. Box 268, 12529; (518) 325-3412. 110 mi. north of New York City at inter-section of Rtes. 22 and 23. Glacé Red Raspberry Soufflé, page 26.

Stony Brook. The Three Village Inn. Dock Road 11790; (516) 751-0555. From Long Island Expressway take Exit 62, north on Nichols Road to Rte. 25A, then turn left at traffic light and follow to Main St. Turn right to inn. Cold Cauliflower Nivernais, page 12.

NORTH CAROLINA

Hillsborough. Colonial Inn. 153 W. King St. 27278; (919) 732-2461. Take I-85 to Exit 164 between Greensboro and Durham and go 1½ mi. to Hillsborough, turning left at King St. light. Country Ham with Red-Eye Gravy and Hush Puppies, page 21.

Tryon. Pine Crest Inn. Box 1030, Pine Crest Lane 28782; (704) 859-9135. From Asheville take I-26 south to Rte. 108 thence to Tryon; turn from Trade St. into New Market Rd. and follow to Pine Crest Lane. Chicken and Rice Ring with Mushroom Sauce, page 22.

OHIO

Burton. Welshfield Inn. 14001 Main Road to Market (U.S. 422) 44021; (216) 834-4164. On U.S. 422 in Welshfield, 300 yards east of intersection with Rte. 700. Poppy Seed Dressing, page 114.

Lebanon. The Golden Lamb. 27 S. Broadway 45036; (513) 932-5065. From I-71 take Exit Rte. 48N, then turn west 3 mi. to Lebanon. From I-75 take Exit Rte. 63E, then turn east 7 mi. to Lebanon. Braised Lamb Shanks, page 102.

OREGON

Gleneden Beach. Salishan Lodge. P.O. Box 118, 97388; (503) 764-2371. On Rte. 101 near Depoe Bay, 90 mi. from Portland. Fillet of Sole Marguery, page 120.

PENNSYLVANIA

Gilbertsville. Jack Gleason's Fagleysville Country Hotel. Swamp Pike, R.D. 1, 19525; (215 Pottstown) 323-1425. From Reading take U.S. 422 to Rte. 100 and turn left; go about 3 mi. then turn right onto Route 73 which becomes Swamp Pike, proceeding about 4 mi. to Fagleysville. From Norristown take U.S. 422 to Limerick, turn right onto Swamp Pike; Fagleysville is 3.9 mi. from stop light in Limerick. Sweet-Sour Zucchini Salad, page 75.

Mt. Joy. Groff's Farm Restaurant. Pinkerton Road, R.D. 3, 17552; (717) 653-2048 — reservations only. From Lancaster take Rte. 283 west to Mt. Joy, about 11 miles. Chicken Stoltzfus, page 13.

New Hope. Logan Inn. Cannon Square 18938; (215) 862-5134. Take New Jersey Turnpike to Exit 10 and follow Rte. 287 to Somerville; at traffic circle take Rte. 202 South to New Hope. Look for memorial cannon. From Philadelphia take I-95 north to Rte. 32, following it to New Hope. Chicken Livers Romanoff, page 48.

SOUTH CAROLINA

Charleston. Sword Gate Inn. 111 Tradd St. 29401; (803) 723-8518. From I-26 take Meeting Street Downtown exit and follow Meeting to Broad. Turn right, then left on Legare St. and left again to Tradd St. Inn will be on right. Cinnamon Breakfast Apples, page 92.

TEXAS

Austin. Erich's. 13614 Highway 71 West 78746; (512) 263-2023. From downtown Austin take I.H. 35 south, then west on Rte. 71 to Bee Cave, ¼ mi. beyond intersection with Ranch Road 620. Wiener-Kalbs Goulash, page 57.

Fort Worth. The Carriage House. 5136 Camp Bowie Blvd. 76107; (817) 732-2873. Mr. Mac's Salad Dressing, page 58.

Jefferson. New Jefferson Inn. 124 Austin St. 75657; (214) 665-2631. From Dallas take I-20 east to Marshall exit then turn north on U.S. 59 to Jefferson. Shrimp Gumbo, page 28.

VERMONT

West Dover. The Inn at Sawmill Farm. P.O. Box 367, 05356; (802) 464-8131. From I-91 take Rte. 9 west to Wilmington; at Wilmington Rte. 100 north to West Dover; entrance just north of village. Roast Duckling au Poivre Vert, page 18.

VIRGINIA

Middletown. Wayside Inn Since 1797. Drawer 255, 22645; (703) 869-1797. From I-81 take Rte. 77 to Rte. 11 South, follow signs to inn at 7783 Main St. From Washington, D.C., take I-66 to I-81; take Exit 77 from I-81 to Rte. 11 South; follow signs to inn at 7783 Main St. Wayside Inn Peanut Soup, page 19.

WASHINGTON

Coupeville. The Captain Whidbey Inn. 2072 West Whidbey Inn Road 98239; (206) OR 8-4097. Take Mukilteo ferry to Columbia Beach, then Rte. 525 north to Coupeville, then Rte. 20 3 mi. north to Penn Cove. Washington Apple Cake, page 126.

WEST VIRGINIA

Berkeley Springs. The Country Inn. 207 S. Washington St. 25411; (304) 258-2210. Northwest of Baltimore and Washington via I-70 and I-270. Take Hancock exit east at U.S. 522, go 6 miles south to junction with Rte. 9. Hot Buttered Rum and Country Inn Apple Sour, page 66.

WISCONSIN

Bayfield. Old Rittenhouse Inn. 301 Rittenhouse Ave. 54814; (715) 799-5765. From Duluth, MN take Rte. 2 eastward 57 mi. to Rte. 13 then take 13 north 13 mi. to Bayfield. Strawberry Consommé, page 74.

Fish Creek. The White Gull Inn. Box 175, 54212; (414) 868-3517. Take I-43 from Milwaukee to Manitowoc, then Rte. 42 to Fish Creek; turn left at bottom of hill to sign of the White Gull Inn. Door County Fish Boil, page 72.

Mequon. Boder's on the River. 11919 N. River Road, 43W, 53092; (414) 242-0335. From Milwaukee take I-43 15 mi. north to Rte. 167, turn west to Rte. 57 then drive north to Freistadt Rd.; turn right to River Rd. Zwiebelkuchen (Onion Pie), page 80.

WYOMING

Lander. Miner's Delight Inn. Box 205, Rte. 62, Atlantic City 82520; (307) 332-3513. From Cheyenne take I-80 west to Rawlins, turn north on U.S. 287 to Lander, then take Rte. 28 to Farson, about 27 mi. (watch for sign to Atlantic City); turn left on a dirt road; 3 mi. into Atlantic City. Manicotti Miner's Delight, page 116.

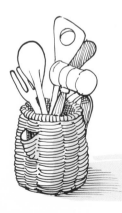

RECIPE INDEX